CRAZY AND A HALF

six insane one-act comedies

by D. R. ANDERSEN

SAMUEL FRENCH, INC.
45 West 25th Street NEW YORK, N.Y. 10010
7623 Sunset Boulevard HOLLYWOOD 90046
LONDON *TORONTO*

ISBN 0 573 62791 6 Printed in U.S.A. #5380

IMPORTANT BILLING AND CREDIT REQUIREMENTS

All producers of CRAZY AND A HALF *must* give credit to the authors of the work in all programs distributed in connection with performances of the Work, and in all instances in which the title of the Work appears for the purposes of advertising, publicizing or otherwise exploiting a production thereof, including, without limitation, programs, souvenir books and playbills. The names of the Authors *must* appear on a separate line in which no other matter appears, immediately following the title of the Work, and *must* be in size of type not less than 50% of the size used for the title of the Work.

Billing *must* be substantially as follows:

(NAME OF PRODUCER)

Presents

CRAZY AND A HALF

D.R. ANDERSEN

"Love is merely a madness and, I tell you,
deserves as well a dark house and a whip as madmen do;
and the reason why they are not so punished and cured
is that the lunacy is so ordinary that the whippers
are in love too."

—William Shakespeare
[*As You Like It* III.ii]

For

Betty Ann

who checks for soft spots in my head

CASTING NOTE

In the six one acts there are a total of six male and six female characters. If all six one acts are performed, six male and six female actors could be cast in the roles.

Another theatrical option would be to double-cast, using only two male and two female actors.

NOTE: The two characters who appear in "I'll Take Manhattan"—the first one act—are also featured in "They Can't Take That Away From Me"—the sixth one act.

STAGING NOTE

The six one-act comedies may, of course, be staged with traditional, realistic sets. (See the scene designs beginning on page 102.)

Another staging option would be to use a few lightweight geometric pieces that can quickly and easily be rearranged to suggest the chairs, desks, and so on needed to meet the requirements of each one act.

Act One: NEW YORK CRAZY

"I'll Take Manhattan"
KIT MARCH
KEENE WINFIELD

"Yes, Sir, That's My Baby"
DR. DELIA CANTOR
IRA POPOFSKY

"In Other Words"
DR. PETER LITTLE
CARLA PICCOLINO

Act Two: CALIFORNIA CRAZY

"Everywhere"
DR. ROBERT KITTLESON
DES RAGE

"You Oughta Be in Pictures"
DR. JANE GOLDIN
CANDY KANE

"They Can't Take That Away From Me"
DR. KIT MARCH
DR. KEENE WINFIELD
TEDDY MOORE
DINAH MOORE

Each scene takes place in the office or therapeutic setting of a different psychiatrist.

Act One: NEW YORK CRAZY

"I'll Take Manhattan"
KIT MARCH
KEENE WINFIELD

"Yes, Sir, That's My Baby"
DR. DELIA CANTOR
IRA POPOFSKY

"In Other Words"
DR. PETER LITTLE
CARLA PICCOLINO

ACT ONE

"I'll Take Manhattan"

(SCENE: The waiting room for several psychiatrists who share office space. There are three doors: one leading to the hallway and two to offices. The waiting room and its furnishings are unremarkable; but several large, old-fashioned, openable windows offer an appealing view of a corner of Manhattan's Gramercy Park area and a large expanse of sky.

TIME: A weekday, a little before seven PM, on a midsummer's evening.

AT RISE, the first thing we notice is the view through the windows: a Tiffany-box-blue sky shimmers as it often does just before a summer sun starts to set.

Suddenly the hallway door swings open and in the doorway standing shoulder to shoulder are KIT MARCH and KEENE WINFIELD, strangers to each other.

KEENE is the one who has turned the doorknob and opened the door; however, because KEENE and KIT are both aggressive, self-important Manhattanites, there is a moment when it isn't certain which one will push to make it through the doorway first. Civilization prevails: KEENE, with a tight smile of superiority, allows KIT to enter ahead of him.

They are both dressed in exquisitely attractive and expensive business clothes, and they are each carrying an exquisitely attractive and expensive briefcase.

There is an agitated urgency in the behavior of both. Studiously ignoring each other, they set their briefcases down at the same time, sit at the same time, cross their legs at the same time, and overly extend their arms (as self-important people do) to look at their exquisitely attractive and expensive wristwatches at the same time.

They both become instantly fidgety, stand, and move discreetly but competitively toward the magazine rack. There are only two magazines: Time *and* Highlights for Children.

KEENE and KIT simultaneously grab for Time*; there is a moment when it appears they might begin a tug-of-war and actually tear the magazine apart.*

But civilization prevails again: KIT, with a tight smile of superiority, allows KEENE to have Time. *KIT picks up* Highlights for Children.

They sit, impatiently thumbing through their respective magazines in synchronous, self-important fashion.

They overextend their arms again to check their watches and sigh audibly and impatiently in unison. This makes them look at each other.)

KIT. What time do you have?

KEENE. Six fifty-nine.

KIT. I have seven.

KEENE. I have six fifty-nine.

KIT. I have seven.

KEENE. My Rolex says six fifty-nine.

KIT. My Rolex says seven.

KEENE. Are you here to see Dr. Freeman?

KIT. Yes.

KEENE. Dr. Louis Freeman?

KIT. Yes.

KEENE. Dr. Louis J. Freeman?

KIT. *(impatiently)* YES. *(with the sudden realization that she may be facing yet another form of Manhattan competition)* Are *you* here to see Dr. Freeman?

KEENE. Yes.

KIT. What time is your appointment?

KEENE. Seven.

KIT. Impossible. I see Dr. Freeman every Tuesday at seven like clockwork.

KEENE. He told me on the phone this morning that he had a cancellation tonight and could take me at seven.

KIT. Well, we'll see when he comes out that door—won't we? *(They stare tensely at the door. KEENE fiddles nervously with his tie. KIT sits rigidly motionless. There is no movement, no sound from Dr. Freeman's office.)* What time do you have now?

KEENE. *(looking at his watch)* I have seven.

KIT. *(looking at her watch)* I have seven-oh-one. *(KIT's self-assurance begins to falter.)* I … I wonder if something's wrong.

KEENE. Why?

KIT. Dr. Freeman is never late. The Greenwich Royal Observatory is more likely to be behind time than Dr. Freeman.

KEENE. That's true but it's only … *(looking at his watch)* seven o'clock and fifteen seconds.

KIT. No, it's not. It's seven o'clock, one minute, and fifteen seconds. He's seventy-five seconds late. *(looking toward Dr. Freeman's door with anxiety, becoming more and more unstrung)* Oh, my God! What if … what if …

KEENE. *(growing increasingly more anxious himself)* What if what?

KIT. What if he's had a stroke! He's alluded to heart trouble more than once. What if he's in there now—slumped in his brown leather club chair … paralyzed!

KEENE. *(following her line of thought)* His pipe dangling from his false teeth … burning ash spilling onto his genital area …

KIT. Unable to reach the phone! Unable to call out for help!

KEENE. Unable to zip his fly!

KIT. I've always found his inevitably open fly strangely endearing. It's embarrassingly Freudian on his part, of course, but it makes him so completely human for me.

KEENE. I know what you mean. And he was so bright … so caring … so eclectic …

KIT. *(horrified)* You said "was." *(KIT flies to the door and, at first, attempts some self-control by knocking gently.)* Dr. Freeman, it's Kit March. Dr. Freeman, are you in there? *(When she gets no answer, she turns the knob. The door is locked but she tries again and again, desperately hoping that perhaps she's not maneuvering the knob correctly. When the door resists all her efforts at opening it, she begins banging on it.)* Dr. Freeman! Please, let me in! I've got to see you!

KEENE. *(knocking in a more gentlemanly fashion on the door, in between KIT's bangings)* Dr. Freeman, it's Keene Winfield. I'm your seven o'clock.

KIT. *(looking through the keyhole)* You are not! I am!

KEENE. *(fighting to get his mouth near the keyhole)* Dr. Freeman, I'm your *emergency* seven o'clock.

KIT. I'm calling Dr. Freeman's service!

KEENE. So am I!

(Each quickly retrieves a cell phone from a pocket. KIT and KEENE simultaneously push their speed dialing buttons. They get busy signals.)

KIT. Stop it!

KEENE. You stop it!

(KIT and KEENE simultaneously push their speed dialing buttons again. They get busy signals.)

KIT. Stop it!

KEENE. You stop it!

(KIT and KEENE simultaneously push their speed dialing buttons yet again. They get busy signals.)

KIT. Stop it!

KEENE. You stop it!

(KIT lets out a piercing, prolonged scream of life and Manhattan frustration, believing, on some level, that this will help make her point with KEENE.)

KIT. *(then quietly)* I honestly need an appointment tonight.

(KEENE jumps up and down in the chair he was sitting on and makes wild grunting sounds—the masculine equivalent of KIT's scream.)

KEENE. *(then quietly)* I honestly do, too.

(Unmoved by KEENE's expression of need, KIT pushes the speed dialing button on her cell phone. KEENE lifts his cell phone as if he is going to enter back into competition with KIT—but he can't muster the wherewithal. He pockets his phone and fiddles nervously with his tie, as he watches KIT with guarded suspicion. Then, suddenly, exhausted from KIT, his personal problems, and the world, he sags into a chair, holding his head in his hands.)

KIT. *(in one urgent gush into the phone)* Hello—this is Katherine March and I'm a patient of Dr. Louis J. Freeman and I have an appointment with him tonight at seven o'clock—as I do every Tuesday night—and I'm in his waiting room right now calling on my cell phone and he's not answering my knock at his door and it's after seven—it's … *(looking at her watch)* seven-oh-four …

KEENE. Oh-three.

KIT. And … What? No. No, that's not possible. I don't care. Do you understand what I'm saying? I don't care! This is Dr. Katherine March. I'm a doctor. An MD. A psychiatrist. *(KIT and KEENE exchange a glance.)* And I want to see Dr. Louis J. Freeman tonight! *(Pause)* Which hospital? *(Pause)* I said—WHICH HOSPITAL? *(Pause—then calmly)* No, I am not crazy. I am crazy and a half. And I will hunt you down like a hound from hell and make your life a living misery if you don't immediately tell me …

(KEENE grabs at the phone but KIT will not let go. They have a wild wrestling match until KEENE finally wrenches the phone from KIT's grasp. KEENE is out of breath but tries to use a reasonable tone.)

KEENE. Hello, this is Dr. Keene Winfield. I apologize for Dr. March's outburst. She is understandably distraught that her appointment seems to have been canceled. I, too, am a patient of Dr. Freeman's and I, too, have an appointment with him tonight at seven. *(Pause)* No—not couple therapy. Two simultaneous individual sessions. *(Pause)* That's right. Now I understand from what I overheard that Dr. Freeman is attending a patient at a hospital. Is that correct? *(Pause)* That is *not* correct. *(Pause)* Dr. Freeman has been … admitted … to a hospital … *(Pause)* And which hospital might that be? *(Pause)* Yes, yes, of course, I understand. But I'm an MD, as well. A psychiatrist myself, in fact. *(KIT and KEENE exchange a glance.)* And, as a professional courtesy, I would think you might be able to … *(Pause. He begins to lose his civilized tone.)* Yes, I know I'm a patient. *(Pause. He loses his civilized tone.)* Well, I'm thrilled Dr. Freeman has a colleague covering for him. Is it by any chance ME? No, I don't want an appointment tomorrow. I want an appointment TONIGHT! *(Pause)* Yes, you do have to take this kind of abuse—you're an answering service!

KIT. *(grabbing the phone from KEENE, speaking in a courteous manner)* Hello, this is Dr. March again. I just want to say … fuck you very much!

(KIT makes a dramatic show of ending the call by pushing a button on the cell phone. KIT and KEENE sit in silent agony. Slowly they they turn to each other and look deeply into each other's eyes.)

KEENE. You're a …

KIT. Uh-huh. You too?

KEENE. Uh-huh.

KIT. Where did you …

KEENE. Exeter, Amherst, Harvard. You?

KIT. Dalton, Bryn Mawr, Johns Hopkins. With honors.

KEENE. You use an eclectic approach in your practice?

KIT. Of course. Strict Freudians are sick. Strict Jungians are sick. In fact, Freud, Jung, and the majority of the now-deceased and some still-living theorists who have contributed to our understanding of the human mind and psychiatry clearly exhibit in their personal lives and professional writings the symptoms of more than one mental disorder described in the current DSMV-IV. Strict anythings need therapy—and usually years of it. In fact, everyone does.

KEENE. Oh, I agree. I agree. I couldn't agree more. And eclecticism is the touchstone of my practice.

(The sky unravels in creamy pale pink and orange ribbons. KIT and KEENE have come to the unspoken understanding that for immediate psychiatric care, they are all they have. Simultaneously, they pull materials out of their briefcases. Each now has a notebook and pen, which he or she uses in the following scene to take notes when in "psychiatrist mode." When in "psychiatrist mode," KEENE and KIT are calm and professional. When in "patient mode," each is urgently frenzied and occasionally hysterical.)

KEENE. *(psychiatrist mode)* Can you tell me what's been going on since your last session?

KIT. *(patient mode)* Angelo left me. And took our Salvador Dali! The bastard! The tall, dark, handsome, narcissistic, withholding, psychotic bastard! He left me—in Tribeca! With a big, fucking white space on the wall where the Salvador Dali used to be!

KEENE. I hear you saying that you're feeling great pain.

KIT. No shit, Sherlock.

KEENE. *(psychiatrist mode)* But judging from your vivid description of him, isn't it a good thing Angelo left you?

KIT. *(patient mode)* Of course not. Angelo is the prize in the Cracker Jack box of my life!

KEENE. *(psychiatrist mode, writing down the phrase)* "The prize in the Cracker Jack box of your life."

KIT. *(in patient mode)* It's why people go crazy.

KEENE. *(psychiatrist mode)* Because they *get* the Cracker Jack prize they want—or because they *don't*?

KIT. *(patient mode)* Both. *(Pause)* Oh, my God! What am I going to do? How am I going to go on without him?

KEENE. *(psychiatrist mode)* I'm wondering if there isn't another way for you to look at things.

KIT. *(patient mode)* NO! THERE IS NOT! (*Pause*) Like what?

KEENE. *(psychiatrist mode)* Maybe … just maybe … life isn't *one* Cracker Jack box—but *many* Cracker Jack boxes. And for every box, there's a prize of love. Different from the one before. And different from the one to come. But, nonetheless … a prize. *(Pause)*

KIT. *(patient mode, with deep sincerity)* That's … brilliant, Dr. … *(He hands her one of his business cards.) (reading the card)* Dr. Winfield. I can honestly draw deep, immediate comfort from the way you've opened up the unfortunate metaphor by which I've been living my life.

KEENE. *(psychiatrist mode)* It's my belief that each of us lives by some metaphor or other—and the metaphor we choose to live by makes all the difference in the world, coloring and shaping the way our lives spin themselves out.

KIT. *(patient mode)* I see now that someday I'll be able to embrace my divorce from Barry and accept my loss of Angelo. A heaviness, a terrible heaviness is falling away from my heart.

KEENE. *(psychiatrist mode, but beginning to betray his own need for help)* So now …

KIT. *(patient mode)* So now I feel as if I could float right out that window and over the city like a balloon in Macy's Thanksgiving Day parade!

KEENE. *(psychiatrist mode)* Well, since you're feeling so much better, perhaps we could … move on to … *(patient mode, anxious, desperate)* ME!

KIT. *(psychiatrist mode)* Yes … yes, of course. How are you feeling … right now … this moment?

KEENE. *(patient mode, quietly)* Agitated. Panicky. Nauseated. I suddenly see that Caroline—who's a musicologist and one of the most sterling people who has ever walked the face of this earth and someone I would never want to hurt in any way imaginable—isn't my Cracker Jack prize in this or any box to come. The realization has been been dawning on me for I don't know how long. But you crystallized it for me tonight, Dr. March. You opened my eyes.

KIT. *(psychiatrist mode)* Well, thank you. *(She hands him one of her business cards.)* But you did the work. It's your insight. Remember that. Give yourself the credit you deserve.

KEENE. *(patient mode)* I will. I will give myself the credit I deserve. But I've got to think of something fast! *You've* got to think of something fast for me!

KIT. *(psychiatrist mode)* Why?

KEENE. Because I'm getting married in four days! This Saturday. In Connecticut. In the garden of my parents' genuinally colonial colonial. With a quartet of musicians playing actual medieval instruments from the actual Middle Ages. My best man is coming from Tokyo. The floral decorations will include clusters of real grapes that are being flown in from Provence. And Caroline, though she graduated summa cum laude from Vassar and is breathtakingly beautiful and can play the harpsichord *and* the clavichord—is not the one! She's not the one! She's not my Cracker Jack prize!

KIT. All I've ever wanted since I divorced Barry—who's a brilliant cardiologist—is to marry Angelo on a Saturday in our loft in Tribeca with our Salvador Dali! Just Angelo, the priest, the minister, Salvador Dali, and me. Balthazar would cater. I lied before. Angelo is the one! He's the one! He's my Cracker Jack prize!

(They sob explosively. As their sobbing subsides, they look at each other.)

KEENE. *(quietly)* Dr. Freeman would know what to do at a juncture like this.

KIT. *(quietly)* He'd even tell us *how* to do it.

(The sky has darkened to a strangely beautiful deep luminescent blue; and the lamps around the office create a cozy, intimate atmosphere. KIT and KEENE look at each other like Hansel and Gretel after discovering that the birds have eaten the breadcrumbs and realizing that neither of them knows the way home.)

KEENE. We've got to figure this out somehow ... alone ... together, Kit.

KIT. It's what he'd want us to do, Keene.

KEENE. But we can't keep wobbling around like demented toy tops.

KIT. *(rallying)* What if we trade full sessions—right here and now?

KEENE. *(rallying, too)* Fifty minutes for you and fifty minutes for me.

KIT. Right!

KEENE. That way we can each have a complete session—uninterrupted by the other's neurotic but completely understandable tantrums and uncontrollable sobbing. You know … this could open up a whole new method of therapy for therapists. It might even lead to a book …

KIT. *(picking up on KEENE's idea, snapping her fingers with excitement)* I've got it: *Couch for Two …*

KEENE. Colon: *When Shrinks Shrink Together*!

KIT. I can see it. I can see it in my head as plain as day. There could even be a movie deal. Who knows?

KEENE. *(with a renewed look of distress)* But for now …

KIT. Yes—for now. We'll both need to stay focused, clear-headed, and …

KEENE. Eclectic.

KIT. And though we are both in need of crisis intervention that will require multiple sessions, as Dr. Freeman has said to me more than once: Even in a single session …

KEENE and KIT. *(almost smiling at each other, echoing the words they've heard from Dr. Freeman)* An epiphany can begin.

KEENE. *(suddenly tense)* Oh, no! I just thought of something.

KIT. What?

KEENE. Suppose somebody shows up. Say a patient for the doctor behind door number two.

KIT. There's a Starbuck's on the corner—and we'll fit right in. The singles are depressed, trying to look absorbed in a book, and the couples are huddled over cups, engaged in intense, tearful conversations.

KEENE. *(with a stunning smile at KIT's wit)* I love Manhattan!

KIT. *(with a stunning smile—right back)* Me, too!

KEENE. *(relieved)* Okay—we're rolling now.

KIT. Couches, ho!

KEENE. *(suddenly tense again)* Oh, no! I just thought of something else.

KIT. What?

KEENE. Who goes first?

(There's a moment of tension. Here we go again: Manhattanites on the battlefield of life and love.)

KIT. *(tensely back)* Oh, my God! I hadn't thought about that. We're both pathologically needy—so from a triage point of view … we're in completely equal distress. *(Pause) (Then frightened:)* I don't know. I honestly don't know who'll go first. Look at me—I'm shaking like a leaf.

KEENE. *(tense)* Look at me—I'm shaking like Sequoia National Forest.

(We wonder for a moment what will happen. Perhaps their tentative strides toward cooperation will have been nothing but talk.)

KIT. *(brightly, being a good sport)* I know! I've got it! Let's flip for it!

KEENE. You're a good sport, Dr. March.

KIT. Thank you for saying so, Dr. Winfield.

KEENE. *(pulls a coin out of his pocket)* Heads—you get shrunk first!

KIT. Tails—you do!

(They laugh briefly but sweetly—suddenly enjoying each other's company.)

KEENE. Here we go!

(KEENE tosses a coin in the air. KIT and KEENE watch it with intense interest when there is a …)

BLACKOUT

"Yes, Sir, That's My Baby"

(SCENE:The office of DR. DELIA CANTOR, a child psychiatrist, on Manhattan's Upper Westside. Colorful bookshelves overflow with books, stuffed animals, toys, and games. In one corner, brightly painted child-sized chairs snuggle up to their matching table. A desk, a desk chair, a file cabinet, and two comfortable overstuffed armchairs complete the room

TIME:A weekday, a little after five PM, on a brilliantly sunny day in early autumn.

AT RISE, DR. CANTOR and IRA POPOFSKY are in the middle of an intense exchange.

DR. CANTOR, with wild hair and off-beat but attractive clothes, has an eccentric manner, yet is highly competent and professional. IRA's clothes are wrinkled and askew, as if he's slept in them. His hair is disheveled and he needs a shave.)

IRA. I can't eat. I can't sleep. I can't sit still long enough at my drawing board to finish anything. I'm desperate. Can't you see I'm desperate?

DR. CANTOR. *(exhausted by IRA, trying to stay polite, managing civility)* Yes.

IRA. I'm so desperate I might do something desperate.

DR. CANTOR. Like what?

IRA. I don't know. Do you have any ideas?

DR. CANTOR. Well, yes I do.

IRA. What?

DR. CANTOR. Grow up.

IRA. That's a terrible thing for a child psychiatrist to say.

DR. CANTOR. It's a terrible thing for a child psychiatrist to have to say—to an adult.

IRA. Okay—that's fair. And I will try to grow up—tomorrow. But what am I going to do *today*?

DR. CANTOR. We've been over this a hundred times.

IRA. Well, then I guess this will make it the hundred and oneth.

DR. CANTOR. *(wearily)* You have to accept the custody settlement.

IRA. I can't.

DR. CANTOR. You have to give up Harry.

IRA. I can't.

DR. CANTOR. And you have to hand him over—today.

IRA. I can't.

DR. CANTOR. Eleanor Roosevelt said, "You must do the thing you think you cannot do."

IRA. And Franklin Roosevelt said, "The only thing we have to fear is fear itself." And he was right. But I still fear fear. And Eleanor was right. But I cannot do the thing I think I cannot do. So what? I should care if the Roosevelts hate me?

DR. CANTOR. Just stop for one minute—and think about Harry.

IRA. Harry is all I do think about. I watch him sleep. I count his eyelashes. I examine every bowel movement he has with scientific fervor.

DR. CANTOR. I'm asking you to stop and think about Harry's emotional well-being.

IRA. Everything I've ever done has been for Harry's emotional well-being. I've taken care of him day and night—from the minute he was born—for five years. We're completely and totally bonded. It's a Vulcan mind- and body-meld. He's part of me. I'm part of him. To be without him would be like not having cable.

DR. CANTOR. I hear you talking about *your* emotional well-being—not Harry's.

IRA. Maybe they're one and the same. *(Trying his best to avoid reality, IRA pulls out his wallet and a long string of photographs safely framed in plastic cascades open.)* Here he is on the day he was born. He was so little. And with all that hair. People immediately said he looked just like me. And when I first held him—it happened. The mother thing. The Konrad-Lorenz- with-the-baby-ducks thing. My life changed in that moment. It was hormonal. I was his daddy and he was my baby—and no force in the universe could ever change that or pull us apart. Here he is in the kitchen falling on his head. Here he is in Central Park, throwing up a dandelion. Here he is on his third birthday with a candle self-inserted up his nose. I'll never forget that day.

DR. CANTOR. And—don't you see?—no one is asking you to forget.

IRA. Yes, someone is. Someone is. *(IRA becomes incoherent from his physical and mental exhaustion, even as he tries to center himself by looking at the photographs.)* Here he's reading *Goodnight, Moon.* Well, really, chewing *Goodnight, Moon.* But experts say that's an important early literacy skill. And here he's playing in the toilet … and here's the time we … and here's when … and here …

(Pause) (IRA's silence is deafening.)

DR. CANTOR. I hear you saying that you're feeling great pain.

IRA. I wasn't saying anything.

DR. CANTOR. Yes, you were.

IRA. Yes, I was.

DR. CANTOR. And I understand what you're going through.

IRA. You can't. Nobody can understand what I'm going through.

DR. CANTOR. Have you tried to develop a support network as I've suggested?

IRA. Well, sort of. The people I talk to on the street have been really understanding. They're aghast at our judicial system when they hear my story.

DR. CANTOR. You talk to strangers on the street?

IRA. Uh-huh.

DR. CANTOR. Are they derelicts?

IRA. Of course they're not derelicts. Well … one was a derelict. *(Trying to reassure her of his mental health, he raises his index finger and says:)* One.

DR. CANTOR. You really have to start taking care of yourself.

IRA. I've tried. I took that meditation class—remember? But I hurt my neck.

DR. CANTOR. You can't give up.

IRA. Oh, I forgot to tell you—I finally looked into a grief workshop.

DR. CANTOR. Good. That's taking a positive step.

IRA. They wouldn't let me in.

DR. CANTOR. Why not?

IRA. They said the only way I could join was if Harry was dead. Can you imagine any human being saying that to another human being? I can't. I can't imagine any human being saying that to another human being.

DR. CANTOR. But there are other more appropriate groups.

IRA. Anyway, I don't want to sit around sharing my deepest feelings with people. I don't even want to sit around sharing my shallowest feelings with people. I don't like people.

DR. CANTOR. That might be a good jumping off point for your own personal therapy.

IRA. Therapy is just a very expensive way to get a free read of the latest issue of *Time* and *Highlights for Children*.

DR. CANTOR. Therapy is a tool for people to use to make richer, more meaningful lives for themselves.

IRA. I know people who have been therapized. They scare me. They're insane. They're spooky. They're pod people. They say things like, "I've learned to stand back and see the endless disappointments in my life as opportunities." Or "I'm reframing what I used to call my mental breakdown as a time of looking inward." Or "I'm choosing to stop living in the unbearable pain of the past and choosing, instead, to live in the unbearable pain of the moment." I don't want to stand back. I don't want to reframe anything. I don't want to live in the moment. (*Pause*) You know what I want.

DR. CANTOR. Let's look at this another way.

IRA. I've already looked at it that way.

DR. CANTOR. *(testing him)* Which way?

IRA. *(lost in desperation, bluffing)* That way. You know—the way you were just about to mention. That way.

DR. CANTOR. *(gently, sincerely, directly)* Should we stop talking then?

(IRA stands up as if he is going to walk petulantly out the door at this question. Instead he walks to the window, gazes out thoughtfully, turns back, and sits in one of the children's chairs.)

IRA. *(quietly, deeply, intensely)* No. I don't want to stop talking.

DR. CANTOR. If you choose, you can tell yourself over and over that you're losing Harry and you can tell yourself over and over that losing him is going to make you miserable—until you're frazzled, sick, and looking like a crazy person.

IRA. *(quietly—able to hear her now)* Am I looking like a crazy person?

DR. CANTOR. Yes. *(IRA puts his arms down on the little children's table that his chair is tucked under and then puts his face down on his arms—like a child at school. He says something but it is muffled and inaudible. DR. CANTOR walks up next to the table. Then, like a gentle teacher, says:)* Pardon. I didn't hear what you said. *(With his head in the same position, he repeats what he said but it is still just as muffled and inaudible as before.)* Can you lift your head up just a little so I can understand you?

IRA. *(lifts up his head and says clearly)* No, I cannot lift my head up just a little so you can understand me.

(He plops his head down again.)

DR. CANTOR. *(sits in one of the little chairs next to IRA)* Well, maybe I can at least finish what I was saying. You can play a CD of misery in your head over and over. Or you can eject the misery CD and put on a CD of hope. *(looking at the wretched IRA)* Or a least a CD of pleasant thoughts. *(still looking at the desperate IRA)* Or, if nothing else, a CD of rainfall.

IRA. *(sweetly)* I don't have a CD player in my head. I don't have a CD player in my apartment. That went with the divorce. And I don't even care. I don't want anything but Harry.

DR. CANTOR. Where is Harry now?

IRA. He's in the waiting room. Mrs. Rosenbloom said she didn't mind looking after him.

DR. CANTOR. Well, at this point, I think we should bring him in. The two of you have got to find a way to say good-bye without the help of state or federal marshals.

IRA. Then it will kill me. Living without the one I love isn't living. *(IRA walks to the door with a sense of doom. He opens the door.)*

Thank you, Mrs. Rosenbloom. Harry, please come in. *(Through the door comes HARRY—an irresistible mutt, good-natured and uninhibited. IRA gazes lovingly at HARRY, who reciprocates with a lick. IRA puts his arms around HARRY and hugs him.)* I've taught him some great tricks. Just watch. *(HARRY may or may not do the tricks—it doesn't matter. IRA says the same things whatever happens.)* Okay. Harry, roll over. *(HARRY does or does not do the trick. IRA gives him a doggy treat that he pulls out of his pocket.)* Good boy. Okay. Now, dance, Harry, dance. *(HARRY does or does not do the trick. IRA gives him a doggy treat that he pulls out of his pocket.)* Thatta, boy. Just one more. Harry, play dead. *(HARRY does or does not do the trick. IRA gives him a doggy treat that he pulls out of his pocket.)* Is this a Ripley's-Believe-It-or-Not moment or what? Can you believe the talent of this dog? *(IRA picks up and hugs HARRY and then, ala Marlon Brando, says:)* He coulda been a contender. *(HARRY licks IRA's face.)*

DR. CANTOR. *(smiles pleasantly)* He loves you.

IRA. Yes, he does. *(in a pleading tone)* So you see what I'm talking about? I'll have nothing left without Harry!

DR. CANTOR. Nothing?

IRA. *(distraught)* WHO WILL SLEEP ON MY HEAD?

DR. CANTOR. Your new wife? *(IRA stiffens.)* You know, I don't think I've ever congratulated you. Congratulations.

IRA. *(weakly)* Thank you.

DR. CANTOR. How was the wedding?

IRA. *(unnerved by this out-of-the-blue question, not knowing what answer might upset her)* Small?

DR. CANTOR. Small weddings are the best.

IRA. We're talking very small. Minute. Microscopic. Practically invisible. Just me and Harry … *(muttering)* and Pam.

DR. CANTOR. And the honeymoon?

IRA. *(unnerved again and uncertain what to answer to appease DR. CANTOR)* Small?

DR. CANTOR. Small honeymoons are the best. Where?

IRA. *(with resignation, no longer attempting to hold back information)* At that summer camp for dogs and their people. In Vermont.

DR. CANTOR. Camp Romp-a-lot.

IRA. Yes.

DR. CANTOR. Where we went.

IRA. Yes.

DR. CANTOR. Did he get ticks?

IRA. No—she did.

DR. CANTOR. Good.

IRA. Delia, please.

DR. CANTOR. No.

IRA. Pretty please.

DR. CANTOR. No.

IRA. Pretty please with sugar on it.

DR. CANTOR. No.

IRA. Why not?

DR. CANTOR. Because who found Harry's pregnant mother?

IRA. You did.

DR. CANTOR. And who nursed her back to health?

IRA. You did.

DR. CANTOR. And who delivered the babies?

IRA. You did.

DR. CANTOR. And who fainted?

IRA. I did.

DR. CANTOR. And who knew instantly that Harry was the keeper?

IRA. You did.

DR. CANTOR. And who footed all the vet bills?

IRA. You did.

DR. CANTOR. And who took him for his psychotherapy sessions with that charming lesbian couple in the East Village?

IRA. You did.

DR. CANTOR. And who named him Harry?

IRA. You … no, wait a minute. We did. Remember I bought that "Name Your Baby" book and we looked through it together and thought about the deep implications of the etymological derivations. Like Felix …

DR. CANTOR. From the Latin meaning "happy, fortunate, lucky."

IRA. Moishe …

DR. CANTOR. From the Bronx meaning "somebody's uncle."

IRA. Harry …

DR. CANTOR. A diminutive of Henry from the Old German meaning "you left me and took my dog with you."

(DR. CANTOR grabs a giant, brightly-colored oversized foam rubber mallet sitting on one of the bookshelves. She bops IRA on the head with it.)

IRA. You got our very expensive and large-considering-it's-Manhattan co-op with a garden on the terrace.

(IRA grabs the matching giant, brightly-colored oversized foam rubber mallet sitting on one of the bookshelves. He bops DR. CANTOR on the head with it. In the following volley of exchanges, they continue to bop each other on the head after each line. The bopping is entirely childlike and playful—like a Punch and Judy puppet show. Something suggests that this "mallet therapy" may have been a loving ritual for them when they were married.)

DR. CANTOR. You got everything worth having!

IRA. I did not!

DR. CANTOR. Yes, you did!

IRA. I did not!

DR. CANTOR. YES, YOU DID! You got a dog and a wife.

IRA. I DID Nnnn … *(The foam-rubber mallet drops limply to his side. IRA comes to a deep and painful realization.)* I did. I got a dog. And a wife.

(DR. CANTOR's foam-rubber mallet drops limply to her side. She sits at the children's table, puts her arms down on the table, and then puts her face down on her arms—like a child at school. She says something but it is muffled and inaudible. IRA walks up next to the table. Then gently says:)

IRA. What did you say, Delia? *(With her head in the same position, she repeats what she said but it is still just as muffled and inaudible as before.)* Can you lift your head up just a little so I can understand you?

DR. CANTOR. *(lifts up her head and says clearly)* No, I cannot lift my head up just a little so you can understand me.

(She plops her head down again.)

IRA. *(sits in one of the little chairs next to DR. CANTOR, tenderly)* You can always get another dog.

DR. CANTOR. *(lifts up her head and says clearly)* Like you got another wife?

(She plops her head down again.) (Pause)

IRA. Delia, I'm sorry.

DR. CANTOR. *(lifting up her head)* Right.

IRA. *(guiltily)* I am. I am. I am. *(looks at HARRY, then at DELIA)* And ... *(looks at HARRY, then at DELIA)* And ... *(IRA looks at HARRY, then at DELIA a final time. There is a long pause. HARRY may or may not go to DELIA and put his face sympathetically in her lap. In fact, HARRY might even stand right beside IRA. Then, as his heart breaks, IRA says slowly:)* And ... I've made up my mind. Nothing could ever possibly change it. *(Pause)* You can have Harry.

DR. CANTOR. What?

IRA. You can have Harry. I won't fight you over him.

DR. CANTOR. Why? Why do you say that now? After all these months.

IRA. I'm choosing to stop living in the unbearable pain of the past and choosing, instead, to live in the unbearable pain of the moment.

(Pause. They look deeply into each other's eyes.)

DR. CANTOR. *(quietly)* Thank you.

IRA. *(quietly)* You're welcome. *(Pause)* Don't forget he gets a heartworm pill on the first day of the month.

DR. CANTOR. *(gently, tenderly)* I know.

IRA. They've got those little stickers you can put right on your calendar to remind yourself to give him a pill or to remind yourself that you gave him a pill or to … oh, I never use those little stickers anyway.

DR. CANTOR. *(gently, tenderly)* I know.

IRA. He prefers the small-dog run at Carl Schurz Park even though he's not a small dog. Of course, he can't go in, but he likes to just sit outside and watch.

DR. CANTOR. *(gently, tenderly)* I know.

IRA. *(IRA goes to HARRY and, with enormous effort not to cry, says:)* Hey, buddy. I'll see you a week from Saturday and we'll chew up a pair of my socks together. Okay? *(IRA hugs HARRY. Then he goes to the door and with his hand on the doorknob says:)* And, Delia, for the one hundred and oneth time—I don't not love you. *(Pauses—then to HARRY)* We'll even make 'em your favorite, big guy—argyles!

(IRA pulls up one pant leg to show HARRY the argyle socks he's wearing. HARRY barks or does nothing. IRA exits and closes the door behind him. Pause. HARRY goes to the door and begins pawing at it as if he wants to go with IRA. DELIA walks to the door, sits down next to HARRY, leans her head against the door, and says quietly to him:)

DR. CANTOR. I know. I know. I know.

BLACKOUT

"In Other Words"

(SCENE: The office of psychiatrist DR. PETER LITTLE on Manhattan's Upper Eastside. It contains the expected desk, desk chair, bookcases, file cabinet, coat rack, table and lamp, and two chairs. The office is tailored and painted in several shades of beige—like taupe, pumpkin seed, and sand. Everything has been carefully attended to—with a fashionable minimalist's touch.

TIME: A weekday morning in winter.

AT RISE, DR. LITTLE is sitting at his desk. He looks at his watch and then picks up the phone and presses a number.)

DR. LITTLE. *(nervously good-humored)* I caught you! I know you're swamped with work. Uh-huh. Uh-huh. Uh-huh. I just feel like I haven't seen you in weeks. *(laughing gently, trying to make the call warm not confrontational)* Oh, that was you coming in at midnight last night and leaving at seven this morning. That was a joke. I know. I know. I know. But whenever I call I either get Mary Ann or your voice mail or ... What? No. No. Nothing important. Okay. Sure. When? Right. Talk to you then. B… *(It's clear the person on the other end of the line has hung up even before DR. LITTLE could say "bye." He hangs the phone up with what just might be a look of dejection. He looks at his watch again, stands, straightens his tie and sports jacket, and walks with modest composure to the waiting room door. He opens the door and calmly says:)* Mrs. Piccolino.

CARLA. *(entering)* Thank you.

(DR. LITTLE closes the door carefully and takes his seat.

CARLA PICCOLINO is dressed and groomed well but as simply and unostentatiously as possible. She speaks and moves as if trying to slip through the world unnoticed. She sits in her customary chair, barely seeming to take up any room.

The initial exchanges between the doctor and patient are contained, small, and quiet. However, there's nothing shy, withholding, or hesitant about their conversation. They've had hundreds like it. Their responses should, in whatever manner possible, indicate true and easy intimacy that doesn't require undue effort.)

DR. LITTLE. How was your week?

CARLA. Good. How was yours?

DR. LITTLE. Good.

CARLA. *(with import)* Christmas.

DR. LITTLE. *(a tiny smile of sympathetic understanding)* Christmas.

CARLA. You got my card?

DR. LITTLE. I did. Thanks.

CARLA. Merry Christmas.

DR. LITTLE. Merry Christmas.

CARLA. You're not Jewish.

DR. LITTLE. I'm not Jewish.

CARLA. I ask you that every year.

DR. LITTLE. You do.

CARLA. *(pleasantly)* Happy New Year.

DR. LITTLE. *(pleasantly back)* Happy New Year.

CARLA. I made turkey.

DR. LITTLE. For Christmas?

CARLA. For Christmas

DR. LITTLE. We had turkey.

CARLA. And lasagna.

DR. LITTLE. We didn't have lasagna.

CARLA. For Vinnie ... his mother ... her lasagna ...

DR. LITTLE. Vinnie's mother made the lasagna?

CARLA. She's dead.

DR. LITTLE. *(making a note in CARLA's file)* That's right. I remember. So you made the lasagna.

CARLA. Like his mother always did ... for Vinnie ... at Christmas. He doesn't know it but I use my own recipe—not hers. I just tell him it's hers.

DR. LITTLE. Did he like the lasagna?

CARLA. He never says if he likes anything.

DR. LITTLE. Have you asked?

CARLA. With Vinnie, you don't ask.

DR. LITTLE. Why?

CARLA. He wouldn't answer.

DR. LITTLE. How *was* the lasagna?

CARLA. I don't know. I never know. He never says.

DR. LITTLE. Did *you* like it?

CARLA. I had a bite. For a bite, it was fine.

DR. LITTLE. What else did you have?

CARLA. Antipasto.

DR. LITTLE. Did you like it?

CARLA. I don't remember.

DR. LITTLE. Are you having trouble with your memory?

CARLA. I remember everything.

DR. LITTLE. *(with a small smile)* Except the antipasto.

CARLA. I remember the antipasto. I don't want to talk about the antipasto.

DR. LITTLE. What do you want to talk about?

CARLA. My life.

DR. LITTLE. What about your life?

CARLA. Is it a dream?

DR. LITTLE. No. *(Pause)* Is what a dream?

CARLA. My life. *(Pause)* I wake up. My hands and legs move. And I say, "Is this a dream?" I feed Tiny. And I say, "Is this a dream?" I make coffee and eggs. And I say, "Is this a dream?" I clean the house. And I say, "Is this a dream?" I wash Vinnie's underwear. And I say, "Is this a dream?" I go shopping in grocery stores with neon lights so bright they burn my eyes. And I say, "Is this a dream?" I stand in the right checkout line. And I say, "Is this a dream?" I take the groceries home. I peel potatoes and scrape my knuckles and I bleed and suck the blood. And I say, "Is this a dream?" I talk to Angie and Vinnie, Jr., when they come home from school. And I say, "Is this a dream?" Vinnie comes home from work. And I say, "Is this a dream?" I feed him supper. And I say, "Is this a dream?" I put the dishes in the dishwasher. And I say, "Is this a dream?" I hear Vinnie talking on the phone and watching wrestling on TV. And I say, "Is this a dream?" I feed Tiny. And I say, "Is this a dream?" I talk to Vinnie about the boat he wants to get next summer. And I say, "Is this a dream?" I watch TV with Vinnie until he falls asleep in his Barcalounger and I help get him to bed. And I say, "Is this a dream?" I take my clothes off and go to bed. And I say, "Is this a dream?" I lie in the dark. And I say, "Is this a dream?" I dream. And I say, "Is this a dream?" I wake up. My hands and legs move. And I say, "Is this a dream?"

DR. LITTLE. No. It is not a dream. I hear you saying that you're feeling great pain.

CARLA. I would prefer it to be a dream. You can wake up from a dream. The pain can end when it's a dream.

DR. LITTLE. *(looking in CARLA's file)* What do we have you on now?

CARLA. Something that starts with P. No, that was at first. I know—it's something that starts with Z. No we changed that. And it's not the D anymore or the W. I remember. Yes, it's the N stuff. Sounds like an eye chart. I have magnificent eyes. I can still read the bottom line. PZDWN.

DR. LITTLE. *(calmly scanning CARLA's file)* And you're still taking four one-hundred-fifty milligram capsules at night?

CARLA. I stopped taking it.

DR. LITTLE. *(concerned but not alarmed and showing no sign of worry)* Why?

CARLA. I don't remember.

DR. LITTLE. Maybe we should think about putting you on another medication.

CARLA. I don't want to be put on another medication.

DR. LITTLE. A wonderful new medication has just come on the market. It may help you deal with the feelings you're struggling with.

CARLA. I'm not struggling anymore. Do you see me struggling?

DR. LITTLE. This new medication might give you just the change of outlook you need.

CARLA. I saw a look cross your face just now. You're bored with me.

DR. LITTLE. No.

CARLA. You are a nice man and you try to hide it.

DR. LITTLE. No.

CARLA. Maybe you've given up on me then. Maybe that's what the look was.

DR. LITTLE. No.

CARLA. You are a nice man. With many patients who have many problems. And now their problems are more interesting to you than mine, which you've heard week after week, year after year.

DR. LITTLE. That's not true. I find your problems very interesting.

CARLA. Well, that's nice of you to say. But then you are a nice man. What else would a nice man say?

DR. LITTLE. Thank you. And you are a nice woman.

CARLA. *(picking up her purse)* How long has it been?

DR. LITTLE. Since what?

CARLA. Since I started seeing you.

DR. LITTLE. *(kindly)* My records show our first session was December. Six years ago.

CARLA. *(shaking her head with despair)* Six years. It seems so hopeless. And then the holidays come and always seem to make things worse.

DR. LITTLE. For many people.

CARLA. Six years ... and where am I, Doctor?

DR. LITTLE. What do you mean, Mrs. Piccolino?

CARLA. All these years later—where am I?

DR. LITTLE. Everyone's progress is different. And most people's progress is painfully, achingly slow. Everyone takes a different path. You're on your own path of personal growth.

CARLA. *(opening her purse)* I can accept that. So tell me what my own path of personal growth is. I don't care how far along the path I am. I don't even care if you say I've fallen into a pothole from which no woman of Italian descent has ever returned. Just tell me what my path is.

DR. LITTLE. To understanding ...

CARLA. *(pulling something out of her purse)* I don't understand.

DR. LITTLE. Mrs. Piccolino, what's going on? Say it! Tell me how I can help!

CARLA. *(reveals a small handgun that she has taken out of her purse and points it at DR. LITTLE—then says intensely)* Make me happy.

(DR. LITTLE manages to hold himself together by grabbing onto his chair.)

DR. LITTLE. I can't do that, Mrs. Piccolino. That's not my job. My job is to help you do that for yourself.

CARLA. *(Throughout the following exchange, she keeps the gun unflinchingly focused on DR. LITTLE.)* After six years, I'm telling you I'm still unhappy—and now it's your job. *(Pause)* Make me happy.

DR. LITTLE. Mrs. Piccolino, please put the gun down.

CARLA. Not until you make me happy.

DR. LITTLE. *(rising, moving toward her)* You are a smart, unhappy person.

CARLA. *(looking at her watch)* Correct. And we've got about forty minutes left to fix things. So you better get busy. *(DR. LITTLE moves toward CARLA, who backs away from him. They circle the office.)*

DR. LITTLE. Tell me what would make you happy.

CARLA. In six years, you don't have a clue?

DR. LITTLE. Just tell me—what would make you happy?

CARLA. I don't know.

DR. LITTLE. Think about what you're doing. Don't make a mistake you'll regret for the rest of your life.

CARLA. I already regret the rest of my life. Everyday is just another fitting for my coffin.

DR. LITTLE. Do you think you're the only person in the world who isn't completely happy, completely satisfied?

CARLA. No, of course not. Do I look like an idiot? Don't you think I know you're not happy either. I see it in your face. In your eyes. I have no idea what it is. That's not my business. But I see it.

(DR. LITTLE tries not to react to this remark—but he reacts. Then he lets his reaction go and stays focused on his patient, like the good and loving doctor that he is.)

DR. LITTLE. Give me the gun, Mrs. Piccolino—and I'll make you happy.

CARLA. It's a trick. I won't give you the gun until you make me happy.

DR. LITTLE. I swear it's not a trick.

CARLA. It is!

DR. LITTLE. It's not!

CARLA. It is!

DR. LITTLE. It's not!

CARLA. It is!

DR. LITTLE. It's not! Have I ever lied to you?

(CARLA pauses to think about this.)

CARLA. No. You have never lied to me. Never.

(She is almost ready to hand over the gun. But before she can make up her mind, DR. LITTLE lunges at her and grabs for the gun. CARLA raises her gun-toting arm straight up in the air to keep it away from DR. LITTLE.

DR. LITTLE reaches his arm straight up to try to grab the gun from her. In this position, they almost look like flamenco dancers in a pose.

As DR. LITTLE tries to snatch the gun and as CARLA tries to hold onto it, they sway, bend, and spin in almost dancerlike fashion across the office.

Suddenly they are no longer the self-contained, small people they've been all their lives.

In the struggle, they fall to their knees and then onto the floor. The gun goes off—and both DR. LITTLE and CARLA lie completely still. It isn't clear if one or both have been shot or killed.)

DR. LITTLE. You shot my diploma!

(DR. LITTLE grabs the gun from CARLA, stands, and surprisingly quickly regains his professional composure. CARLA, still on the floor, buries her head in shame.)

CARLA. *(with deepest regret)* Oh, my God. What have I done? What have I done to the only person on the face of this earth who treats me with respect? *(She wraps her arms around DR. LITTLE's legs.)* Forgive me, Dr. Little. Forgive me. I honor and respect you. You have done more for me than the Family—and I mean the entire Family. Are you hearing what I'm saying? I'll go now. I just need to know you forgive me.

(DR. LITTLE tries to move back to his desk and drags CARLA with him as he does so.)

DR. LITTLE. I forgive you, Mrs. Piccolino, but you're not going anywhere. Your session isn't over.

CARLA. I don't care about the session. Keep the money. I'll leave early. I only care about you. I can't bear to leave thinking that you think that I'm ... I don't know what ...

DR. LITTLE. Your session is not over. You demanded that I make you happy—remember?

CARLA. I don't know what came over me. I wasn't myself. Please give me some more of those Zs—or whatever you want me to take. I think they were round and white. No, no—maybe they were oblong and pink. I don't care. The dry mouth, the dizziness, the constipation—they're nothing! I'll drink Pine Sol—if you want me to. Whatever you say. Give me the whole bottom row of the eye chart! PZDWN. Please, Dr. Little! Please! Let me make it up to you!

DR. LITTLE. You don't need medication. You never needed medication.

CARLA. I'm so sorry. I'm so sorry I'm sick to my stomach. *(Still holding on to DR. LITTLE, she pulls an airsickness bag out of her purse—just in case.)* I always carry an airsick bag from Continental in my purse. Make me say a Hail Mary, Dr. Little. I don't care if you're not a priest. I don't care if you're not a Catholic. Make me say a thousand Hail Marys! Make me say a million Hail Marys! I deserve it. I deserve it and more. Make me wear a hair shirt. Drive arrows through me like Saint Sebastian. Make me attend to the sick and dying. There's no one sick and dying in our neighborhood—but if you want me to, I'll go to Lourdes.

DR. LITTLE. Mrs. Piccolino, let me go.

CARLA. Of course. I'm sorry. I'm so sorry. I know where you can get those pants pressed free. And they do impeccable work. Impeccable. *(She hands him a business card from her purse.)* Just say Carla Piccolino sent you.

DR. LITTLE. Mrs. Piccolino, get off the floor.

CARLA. Whatever you say, Doctor.

(She rises to her feet.)

DR. LITTLE. You said you wanted me to make you happy.

CARLA. *(adjusting her hair and makeup in a compact mirror)* I was out of my mind. I was crazy.

DR. LITTLE. No, you were not. *(He raises the gun and points it at her. He keeps it aimed ominously at her throughout the following exchanges— waving it at her when she seems to forget its lethal presence.)* Mrs. Piccolino, I'm going to make you happy.

(As earlier DR. LITTLE was truly shocked at the turn of events, so now is CARLA aghast.)

CARLA. DR. LITTLE!

DR. LITTLE. Turn around.

CARLA. How will my murder solve anything? Yes, it will make me happy. But only for a minute. There's an afterlife. An eternal afterlife. Probably with laundry. Do you want me to be miserable washing and ironing and thinking of this moment forever and ever in the eternal afterlife?

DR. LITTLE. Walk straight ahead.

CARLA. No—not the windows! Don't make me jump! I'm terrified of heights. If you have to do it, give me pills and alcohol and Frank Sinatra records. You know what I mean? We're almost like friends, Dr. Little—you and I after all these years. Don't do anything to hurt me.

DR. LITTLE. This is going to tear the very the heart out of you.

CARLA. *(with quiet dread)* What are you going to do to me?

DR. LITTLE. You told me you wanted me to make you happy.

CARLA. *(hysterical)* I exaggerated! I don't want you to make me happy. I want to be just what I've been all the time I've been seeing you—miserable. I'll be more comfortable that way.

DR. LITTLE. *(still with the gun focused on her)* Well, I won't. *(ominously)* You went right up to the brink today, Mrs. Piccolino.

CARLA. *(terrified)* I did! I did! I went right up to the brink today!

DR. LITTLE. And when love pushes you right up to the brink—jump!

CARLA. Jump?

DR. LITTLE. Say what your heart is shouting or you will die of the silence!

CARLA. *(trying to calm herself)* Don't do this, Dr. Little. Whatever it is—don't do it. I have a husband and two children. I don't see them very often and I have unresolved conflicts with each of them. We're completely dysfunctional and at least two of us are currently under psychopharmacological care. But I have a husband and two children!

DR. LITTLE. *(quietly intense, aiming the gun at her head)* Pick up that phone.

CARLA. *(trying to stay calm)* Anything you say. But if you try to strangle me with the cord, don't leave marks. I have a friend, a semi-celebrity Vegas headliner, who shall remain nameless. Her second husband tried to strangle her with a phone cord. She only wears turtlenecks now. Even in the summer. Should I call 911?

DR. LITTLE. No.

CARLA. Information?

DR. LITTLE. No.

CARLA. The pharmacy in the building?

DR. LITTLE. No.

CARLA. Then who?

DR. LITTLE. Call Vinnie.

CARLA. Vinnie Piccolino?

DR. LITTLE. Your husband.

CARLA. Don't ever call him Vinnie in public. He says it makes him sound like a … well, you know… a character on HBO. Call him Vincent—please.

DR. LITTLE. Call Vincent Piccolino—right now. Or else.

CARLA. He tells me never to call him at work unless it's an emergency.

DR. LITTLE. This is an emergency.

CARLA. I'm fine. Look at me. I'm better than when I walked in here six years ago.

DR. LITTLE. Call him!

CARLA. Oh, Dr. Little, this is a terrible mistake.

DR. LITTLE. Pick up that phone—right now!

CARLA. *(making the telephone call)* Vincent Piccolino, please. It's his wife. That's right. His wife. Mrs. Carla Angelina Piccolino. Social security number 549-78-2907. My mother's maiden name was Benvenuto. Thank you. *(Pause)* Thank God we have a mausoleum all picked out.

(DR. LITTLE has pressed the button for the speaker phone feature so we can clearly hear VINNIE—er, VINCENT—on line. His voice has a strong, sexy, masculine, blue-collar, very Italian sound.)

VOICE OF VINNIE. Carla, I told you never to call me here.

CARLA. Except in an emergency.

VOICE OF VINNIE. What's the emergency?

CARLA. I don't know.

VOICE OF VINNIE. We'll talk about it at home tonight.

DR. LITTLE. *(whispering into CARLA's ear so VINNIE won't hear)* Ask him what he thought about your lasagna.

CARLA. *(shakily at first)* What did you think about my lasagna?

VOICE OF VINNIE. What? Speak up. I can't hear what you're saying.

CARLA. *(a little stronger)* What did you think about my lasagna?

VOICE OF VINNIE. Carla, are you out of your mind?

CARLA. *(again at DR. LITTLE's prompting)* Did you like my lasagna, Vincent?

VOICE OF VINNIE. What lasagna?

CARLA. *(increasingly, CARLA is taking over)* My Christmas lasagna.

VOICE OF VINNIE. I don't remember. That was a week ago.

CARLA. Did you like my New Year's lasagna?

VOICE OF VINNIE. I don't know. What was to like? It was lasagna.

CARLA. So you're saying you eat my lasagna meal after meal, year after year—and you don't know what it tastes like?

VOICE OF VINNIE. It tastes like lasagna.

DR. LITTLE. *(prompting CARLA)* Ask him if it tastes good or if it tastes like shit.

VOICE OF VINNIE. Carla, who was that? I'll kill that guy. Who was it? I'll murder him.

CARLA. It was … Father Peter.

VOICE OF VINNIE. Forgive me, Father. I thought you were one of those hotline guys. Carla runs up a mother-fu … *(VINNIE catches himself just in time.)* A Holy Mother of a bill every month on horoscope and tarot card and psychic and God-knows-what-else hotlines.

CARLA. Once in a great while I call for some peace of mind. Is that a crime?

VOICE OF VINNIE. You should go to church like you are now for some peace of mind.

CARLA. I learned a lot from the tarot card hotline this week, Vincent.

VOICE OF VINNIE Like what?

CARLA. You know.

VOICE OF VINNIE. You're talking about that in front of a priest?

CARLA. *(with superiority)* He thinks it's nothing to be ashamed of.

(DR. LITTLE and CARLA exchange pleasantly playful looks—they've never talked about that subject.)

VOICE OF VINNIE. You told a priest?

CARLA. I'm not calling to talk about that.

VOICE OF VINNIE. Good because we don't talk about that.

CARLA. Father Peter urged me to call and ask you one question before he helps me find an underground railroad for abused wives.

VOICE OF VINNIE. An underground railroad for abused wives? You're crazy. Get home. Right now. Take one of your pills. Call your head doctor. Ask him what color pill to take.

CARLA. *(quietly)* Vinnie, do you like my lasagna?

VOICE OF VINNIE. What?

CARLA. *(quietly)* Do you like my lasagna

VOICE OF VINNIE. I don't understand why ...

CARLA. I'm going to ask you for the last time and then I'm going to kill myself or somebody else ...

VOICE OF VINNIE. Always kill somebody else, honey. And call me first.

CARLA. Well?

VOICE OF VINNIE. *(Something in his voice betrays deep emotion about the lasagna and more.)* I love your lasagna, Carla.

CARLA. *(touched)* You never said that before.

VOICE OF VINNIE. But I did now.

CARLA. *(quietly)* You really love my lasagna?

VOICE OF VINNIE. Yes, I do. I know it isn't Mama's recipe. And I like it better.

CARLA. *(overwhelmed with emotion)* Thank you, Vincent. I just had to hear it. Thank you very much. I just had to hear the words.

DR. LITTLE. *(whispering to CARLA)* Anything else?

CARLA. No.

DR. LITTLE. Say good-bye.

CARLA. Good-bye, Vincent. I love you.

VOICE OF VINNIE. Good-bye, Carla. I love your lasagna. *(PAUSE. CARLA hangs up the phone and looks at DR. LITTLE as if he is a saint, which he is.)*

CARLA. *(taking his hand and kissing it)* I don't know what to say, Dr. Little. Except you are a saint and thank you.

DR. LITTLE. You're welcome, Mrs. Piccolino. *(CARLA picks up her belongings and walks to the door.)*

DR. LITTLE. Next week?

CARLA. Like always.

(She smiles beatifically and exits. DR. LITTLE. closes the door. He pauses for just a moment and then goes to the phone and presses the buttons to make a call.)

DR. LITTLE. *(with the same confident tone he's used with CARLA)*

Hi—it's me again. I know I just called. Uh-huh. Uh-huh. Uh-huh. *(He pulls the bullet out of his diploma and tosses it in the air like a coin. Then he pulls the gun out of his pocket—he had stashed it there at an earlier moment during the phone call. He places the gun on the desk in front of him.)* Yes, there is a reason. A good reason. When we talked a little while ago, I said I was calling about nothing in particular. But I lied. The truth is … I needed to hear your voice. No, that's not all. I don't care if there is another call coming in. Let it buzz or blink or whatever the hell it does. *(DR. LITTLE twirls the gun in the air like he's seen in cowboy movies.)* And close your door—okay? Are you closing it? Is it closed? Good. I know. I know. I know. You're right. This isn't like me—but we're all full of surprises, aren't we? So why don't you sit down. Are you sitting down? Good. Why? I'll tell you why: I'm on the brink about something ...

END ACT ONE

Act Two: CALIFORNIA CRAZY

"Everywhere"
DR. ROBERT KITTLESON
DES RAGE

"You Oughta Be in Pictures"
DR. JANE GOLDIN
CANDY KANE

"They Can't Take That Away From Me"
DR. KIT MARCH
DR. KEENE WINFIELD
TEDDY MOORE
DINAH MOORE

ACT TWO

"Everywhere"

(SCENE: The office of DR. ROBERT KITTLESON, located in Hollywood, is very unHollywood. It seems small and cramped. Files are sitting in piles all around. A file cabinet is so full it can't be closed. Bookshelves overflow. DR. KITTLESON's desk is dominated by a computer and more files. A table along one wall has a small lamp and a coffee maker. An old sofa and chair complete the office. All in all, the office is reminiscent of the college dorm room of a brilliant student with no social life.

TIME: A weekday morning, on a rainy spring day.

AT RISE, DR. ROBERT KITTLESON is opening the door to his waiting room. Plain and nondescript, perhaps wearing wire-rim glasses, DR. KITTLESON exudes intelligence and a complete lack of whimsy. He was, no doubt, his high school valedictorian, captain of the debating club, and dateless on prom night.)

DR. KITTLESON. Mr. Rage.

DES. *(entering like a star)* Dr. K! How's shit?

(DR. KITTLESON appears instantly annoyed by DES and his behavior and, in fact, is annoyed and fed up with him as a patient. DES RAGE, lead singer in his band Discharge, is dressed in upscale grunge with cowboy boots. He speaks with a working-class British accent. He walks as if he's suffering from severe hemorrhoids.)

DR. KITTLESON. *(closing the door)* Why are you walking like that?

DES. Bloody hemorrhoids! Goddamned, bloody, fuckin' hemorrhoids!

DR. KITTLESON. Mr. Rage, I have asked you repeatedly over the months not to use that kind of language in our sessions.

DES. *(sweetly)* I'm goddamned, bloody, fuckin' sorry, but that's the goddamned, bloody, fuckin' way I talk. Please forgive me, Mother Teresa.

DR. KITTLESON. She's dead. And that's not funny. Mother Teresa is one of my personal saints. She left the world a better place. She didn't leave behind a trail of filthy rock song lyrics as her legacy.

DES. I suppose that was meant to twist my piercings?

DR. KITTLESON. If it worked, yes.

DES. *(sitting on the sofa—with difficulty)* Goddamned, bloody, fuckin' hemorrhoids! *(DR. KITTLESON starts to chastise DES again.)* I'm sorry, mate. But I feel like there's an electric guitar up my arse.

DR. KITTLESON. Are you sure there isn't?

DES. *(laughing)* You're in a humorous mood this mornin'.

DR. KITTLESON. Quite the opposite, Mr. Rage …

DES. The name is Des, mate—remember?

DR. KITTLESON. Yes, I remember. Des …

DES. What is it, Bobby boy?

DR. KITTLESON. For the purposes of this session, my name is Dr. Kittleson. Not Dr. K. Not Bobby boy. Not mate. Dr. Kitttleson.

DES. Aye, alright then. If that's the way you want it.

DR. KITTLESON. That's the way I want it.

DES. Forgive me for sayin' so, but it sounds to me like you're the one with the electric guitar up your bum.

DR. KITTLESON. Stop it right this minute or I'll call our session to an end now!

DES. Oh, go bollocks! You wouldn't do that to a poor, pathetic lad down on his luck in goddamned, bloody, fuckin', hemorrhoid-suckin' Hollywood. Hey, there's poetry there for fuck's sake!

(DES pulls out a small notebook and pencil and jots down the phrase.)

DR. KITTLESON. Mr …

DES. Des. I can't hear a thing you say to me if you call me Mr. Rage.

DR. KITTLESON. Des, I'm going to be very straight with you today.

DES. Then you're the only one in this whole cokin'-smokin'-tokin' burg who is.

DR. KITTLESON. I don't want you to leave this office with any misconceptions.

DES. My whole life has been one long misconception, startin' with my misconception by a drunken barmaid who gave me so-called birth in an alley behind a pub in some piss pot of a place I don't even know the name of.

DR. KITTLESON. Yes, I remember.

DES. Spiralin' down from the giddy height of that misconception, I landed like Oliver fuckin' Twist in a series of homes for wayward boys run by wayward pedophiles.

DR. KITTLESON. Your early years were tragic.

DES. No, they were not tragic. They were nothin'. Tragic you can remember with photograph albums filled with yellowin' pictures of yellowin' people. But nothin' … you can do nothin' with but live like somebody lives who was born without an arm or a leg. But onto cheerier subjects—did you hear the latest? What's the difference between a fridge and a poof?

DR. KITTLESON. That is quite enough.

DES. *(quietly)* Yes, it is. It's quite enough. *(sprawling out as comfortably as he can on the sofa)* It's quite enough … ahh … *(getting comfortable, in fact, so comfortable that he starts to fall asleep)* Yes … it's quite … enough … for a lifetime … *(DES begins to snore lightly.)*

DR. KITTLESON. Please do not fall asleep. *(DES snores sweetly, a little louder.)* I said—please do not fall asleep. *(DES is now happily in dreamland. DR. KITTLESON goes to him and taps him on the shoulder with a finger.)* Wake up. *(DES is falling deeper and deeper asleep. DR. KITTLESON taps him a little harder. He responds slightly, as if bothered by a fly.)* Wake up. *(DR. KITTLESON shakes DES by the shoulders.)* I said—wake up! *(DES is not waking up. DR. KITTLESON sits on the sofa to get a better grip on DES, takes him firmly by the shoulders, and shakes him vigorously. DES's head and upper body bob and dip and shake like a child's puppet. DR. KITTLESON is frustrated and at the end of his rope.)* Wake up or I'll call the police!

DES. *(starting to come alert)* A lovely band—the Police—a bit behind the times—but a lovely band.

DR. KITTLESON. Now stand up.

DES. I can't—not with these you-know-what up my you-know-what.

DR. KITTLESON. *(helping him to stand)* You don't have to move. You just have to stand. There—now you're standing.

(DES slumps over the back of the sofa.)

DES. Oww! That hurt my willy. Now I've got a sore bum and an achin' willy and friends. I might have to sue you.

DR. KITTLESON: Stand up.

DES. I'm tryin'.

(DES struggles to rise from his slumped position over the back of the sofa, slipping and sliding before finally making it upright. From the pot of a coffee maker on a side table, DR. KITTLESON pours coffee into a cup and hands it to DES.)

DR. KITTLESON. Here.

DES. Styrofoam. That's all you think o' me?

DR. KITTLESON. Drink it.

DES. I pray to all the unholy saints of inebriation—make it vodka.

DR. KITTLESON. Yes, hot, black vodka straight from my own patron saint—Mr. Coffee.

DES. *(taking a sip)* Now can I sit down?

DR. KITTLESON. Not until you hear what I have to say.

DES. Can I lean a little on somethin'?

DR. KITTLESON. *(with a frustrated sigh)* Yes, you can lean against the wall. *(DR. KITTLESON helps DES over to a clear space of wall and helps him lean against the wall. Then solemnly:)* Des, this is our last session.

DES. *(suddenly paying attention; this is a matter of grave importance to him)* That's bollocks, that is! I pay you and I pay you well.

DR. KITTLESON. This doesn't have anything to do with payment.

DES. And I've never brought any illegal substances into this office on my person.

DR. KITTLESON. Yes, you have.

DES. Once and only once. Our first meetin'. And I asked politely if you wanted a line. I'm not a selfish man.

DR. KITTLESON. And this doesn't have to do with your continuing struggle with substance abuse.

DES. Speakin' of abuse, this black vodka's burned off half my fuckin' tastebuds.

DR. KITTLESON. Good.

DES. *(not meaning it in the least)* You're a madman. I knew it all along. You're a madman.

DR. KITTLESON. You have been coming to me for seven months …

DES. And a lovely seven months they've been.

DR. KITTLESON. And within minutes of the beginning of every session, you have fallen asleep.

DES. *(sincerely)* Not the first month. The first month I stayed wide awake every minute of every session. I was figurin' out who you are. And I figured out you are the livin', breathin' spirit of the Girl Guides. Walkin' here among us without your uniform. And, you may not know it—but that's high praise comin' from the likes o' me.

DR. KITTLESON. *(unmoved by his sincerity)* But every month since then all you've done is drift off to sleep in each and every one of our sessions. That is not what therapy is for. Therapy is for talking. Therapy is for thinking. Therapy is for resolving internal and external conflicts. Therapy is not for sleeping.

DES. Aren't you the very one who told me—and dead serious, too—that each and every person's therapy takes a very different road from each every other person's therapy?

DR. KITTLESON. I did.

DES. Well, some blokes take the high road and some blokes take the low. And I'm a bloke that's just tailor-made for the low.

DR. KITTLESON. *(trying to remain in control)* But sleep is not permissible on any of the roads.

DES. Everyone I know tells me I'm a different man since I've been comin' to see you.

DR. KITTLESON. That would be flattering if we had ever achieved anything together—awake. But all I do is sit and watch you sleep for fifty minutes. Then I wake you up, tell you your session is over, you hand me an illegible check and leave.

DES. Sometimes it feels like a whole heavenly night.

DR. KITTLESON. *(more and more agitated)* Can't you understand this isn't why I became a doctor—to sit and watch a patient sleep? I became a doctor, a psychiatrist, to help people discover what they might not be able to discover on their own, to make their lives better, easier, more comfortable, more complete.

DES. Then shag and bugger me till I'm blue if that's not exactly what you've done for me! Can't you see the change in me?

DR. KITTLESON. No, I cannot. I cannot see the change in you. You're never awake long enough for me to notice anything about you. I've been trying to talk to you about this for weeks. But you're out like a light before I even get the chance to find out what's been going on with you. Do you understand this is not what I was trained to do? I've done my best to get through to you, but I can't go on like this anymore. I'm at the end of my rope—no, I'm off the end of my rope—I'm just hanging suspended by nothing. Our sessions are complete and utter failures in every possible way. I accept full responsibility for the problem—but our relationship has got to end and end now!

(Shaking with emotion, DR. KITTLESON is as distraught as he has ever been in his personal life or professional career.)

DES. You know what I hear?

DR. KITTLESON: No, I don't. I don't know what you see or think or feel or hear … or anything!

DES. *(quietly)* I hear you sayin' that you're feelin' great pain.

DR. KITTLESON. I am.

DES. And do you know—that makes me sick, sick at my very heart to think that I've been the cause of that great pain?

DR. KITTLESON. I'm sorry. Let's not talk about this any longer. Let's just shake hands and say good-bye.

DES. *(now distraught himself)* I can't do that! I refuse to do that! I'll fuckin' wither away and die without you!

DR. KITTLESON. You've survived three overdoses, several nasty divorces, two bottom-of-the-charts CDs—in a row!—and some ugly press about a replacement drummer for *Discharge*. I think you'll survive not sleeping in my office.

DES. Those were low remarks and not worthy of you.

DR. KITTLESON. I'm sorry. It was wrong of me to say those things. But I'm at a breaking point. Leave—please leave. Before I say something else we'll both regret.

DES. Do you want me to go before you hear the song I've been writin' for you, writin' about you really?

DR. KITTLESON. Surely you know by now that false flattery will get you nowhere with me.

DES. Those, those are stingin' words. Those are words skeined and tangled with nettles to burn my flesh.

DR. KITTLESON. They were meant to be honest words. Please go.

DES. Can't I sing it for you before I go?

DR. KITTLESON. *(impatiently)* If you promise to go and go for good afterwards.

DES. I promise to do anything you tell me to do.

DR. KITTLESON. *(dismissively)* Alright. Then sing the song. And be prepared to leave.

(DES speak–sings the words of the song. It's a sincere, love song—not the usual DES RAGE number.)

DES.

The world's got no corners anymore
Don't know why
Just no edges, no spaces
To rest my head
The world's got no rooms anymore
Can't say why
Just no timbers, no softwood
To make my bed

The world's got no walls anymore
Don't know why
Just no doorways, no places
Where I can lean
The world's got no shape anymore
Can't say why
Just no angles, no ridges
For me to hide between

But there is shelter in you
I have shelter in you
There is shelter for me
Everywhere in you

The world's got no time anymore
Don't know why
No time for deep knowing
No time for true questing
The world doesn't care anymore
Can't say why
No sweet dreaming for me
No heart's resting

But there is shelter in you
I have shelter in you
There is shelter
There is shelter
There is shelter for me
Everywhere in you

(DR. KITTLESON is stunned.)

DES. I've never trusted anyone. I've never loved anyone. I imagine, I never will, never can. And in this cold, dark, endless night—my life—I've never known a moment o' peace, a moment o' rest—with anyone anywhere. Except here—with you. *(Pause)* Can I stay today? *(Pause)* Can I stay?

DR. KITTLESON. *(in a whisper of glad astonishment)* Yes.

DES. *(sprawling out on the sofa)* What do you think of my new song? It's rough. I know it's rough. But what do you think of it? *(He is already on the verge of sleep.)*

DR. KITTLESON. It's … *(DES begins to snore lightly.)* So beautiful … *(DES is breathing more and more deeply as sleep embraces him.)* So surprising … *(DR. KITTLESON yawns a great, satisfying yawn. DES snores deeply. He is all the way to dreamland. DR. KITTLESON's head bobs gently down to his chest—he, too, is falling asleep.)* So … comforting …

(The two are going to have a very peaceful session. DR. KITTLESON and DES are now both soundly and happily asleep.)

BLACKOUT

"You Oughta Be in Pictures"

(SCENE: The office of psychiatrist DR. JANE GOLDIN is located on the third floor of a professional building in Santa Monica. It is impeccably decorated with tailored restraint, so tailored as to be severe.

TIME: A weekday, around noon, on a lovely day in late summer.

AT RISE, DR. JANE GOLDIN is methodically replacing patient files in a file cabinet. She is wearing a dark, well-tailored suit. Her hair is pulled back neatly and somewhat severely in a bun. She is wearing dark-rimmed bifocals. All in all, she has the air of a very serious, focused, competent professional. A buzzer buzzes, announcing the arrival of a patient. DR. GOLDIN calmly and collectedly closes the file cabinet drawer, walks to, and opens the door to the waiting room. Stepping into the doorway is a person-sized bunny holding a bouquet of helium-filled balloons.)

DR. GOLDIN. *(unflinchingly)* Ms. Wong?

CANDY. *(stepping into the room, extending her arm, and shaking paws)* Hi. I know this seems kind of weird but there's actually a logical explanation.

DR. GOLDIN. *(betraying no emotion)* I'm sure there is. Please come in. You might want to hang your balloons on the coat rack and make yourself comfortable right over here. *(CANDY attaches the balloon bouquet to the coat rack, hangs her shoulder bunnybag on a hook, and sits in the chair indicated by DR. GOLDIN, crossing her legs with some difficulty in the slightly bulky costume.)*

CANDY. Thanks. Now let's see—where should I start?

DR. GOLDIN. *(taking notes)* First, I need to find out a few basics.

CANDY. Do you mind if I smoke? And don't worry I'm completely flame retardant.

DR. GOLDIN. Actually, I do mind.

CANDY. Do you mind if I chew gum?

DR. GOLDIN. Not at all.

CANDY. Do you have any?

DR. GOLDIN. No, I'm afraid I don't.

CANDY. A Life Saver?

DR. GOLDIN. Sorry.

CANDY. I try not to smoke or eat refined sugar either except at a party when I don't want to hurt somebody's feelings or in times of extreme anxiety like this.

DR. GOLDIN. *(all business)* I understand. Now to begin with, you told me on the phone that your name is Anastasia Wong. Can you spell that for me?

CANDY. I can spell it for you—but it's not my name.

DR. GOLDIN. But on the phone …

CANDY. I know but I forgot to think of a name before I called you and then when you asked me my name I didn't want to give you my real name and I suddenly thought of the name Anastasia from the movie *Anastasia*, starring Ingrid Bergman, and the name Wong from the movie *The World of Suzie Wong*, starring William Holden—not as Suzie Wong, of course, that was Nancy Kwan though originally the role was to have been played by France Nuyen—and I didn't want to give you my real name in case I got cold feet and decided not to show up and that way you couldn't charge me or take me to small claims court or anything.

DR. GOLDIN. I see. Well, what *is* your real name?

CANDY. Candy Kane.

(She walks to DR. GOLDIN and looks over her shoulder at what she's writing.)

DR. GOLDIN. *(writing it down)* Candy Kane.

CANDY. *(spelling it)* Capital C little A-N-D Y space capital K little A-N-E.

DR. GOLDIN. Thank you.

(CANDY returns to her chair.)

CANDY. You're welcome and I only looked to make sure you spelled it right, not because I don't trust you, but because there are so many ways to spell *Candy* like it could be capital C little A-N-D-I with a little smiley face in the circle above the I but I think that's pretentious—don't you?—or you could spell it capital K little A-N-D-Y and that's really, well, I don't even know the word for it and then *Kane,* well, you could spell it capital C little A-N-E but then it would sound like the name of a drag queen and I don't think I look like a drag queen—do you think I look like a drag queen?

DR. GOLDIN. It's not a good idea for a therapist to comment on …

CANDY. No—don't answer that because on some days I know I do look like a drag queen but it's a fashion statement and that's not why I'm here anyway.

DR. GOLDIN. But your real name is Candy Kane.

CANDY. I know everybody says it's weird or something but my real, actual, true name is Candace and my real, actual, true biological dad, whose name was Arthur Bergen, is no longer living so I was Candace Bergen for three years of my life but then my mother remarried and my stepfather's real, actual, true name is Herbert Kane and he adopted me and I love him alot alot alot—but we weren't too close or anything like that—and that's not why I'm here either but my real, actual, true name is Candy Kane.

DR. GOLDIN. Your age.

CANDY. Thirties.

DR. GOLDIN. Can you be more specific?

CANDY. Kind of middle-ish thirties.

DR. GOLDIN. Your address.

CANDY. Hollywood.

DR. GOLDIN. Can you be more specific?

CANDY. Do I have to?

DR. GOLDIN. No, it's not absolutely necessary.

CANDY. Okay. One-forty-two Cynthia Street. Apartment three R. West Hollywood.

DR. GOLDIN. I thought you didn't want to give me your address.

CANDY. I didn't but I changed my mind and I change my mind alot alot alot.

DR. GOLDIN. What is your marital status?

CANDY. None.

DR. GOLDIN. I mean are you single or married or living with someone?

CANDY. No.

DR. GOLDIN. Did I leave out a category?

CANDY. Well, see, it's complicated.

DR. GOLDIN. Maybe we can pursue that later.

CANDY. Okay.

DR. GOLDIN. What is your occupation, Ms. Kane?

CANDY. Please call me Candy.

DR. GOLDIN. Alright. What is your occupation, Candy?

CANDY. I do just about everything.

DR. GOLDIN. Can you be …

CANDY. More specific?

DR. GOLDIN. Please.

CANDY. I work part-time as a volunteer at the ASPCA because I feel strongly about animal rights alot alot alot and, in fact, I belong to Fur-No-More and I know what you're thinking because everybody kids me about it but this isn't real rabbit fur and I don't think wearing a bunny costume is in any way demeaning to rabbits and actually I'm an actor and I'm just finishing a screenplay I've written especially for myself though that's not the way I make my living either.

DR. GOLDIN. So you *don't* make your living as an actor or as a screenwriter?

CANDY. No.

DR. GOLDIN. What *is* your occupation?

CANDY. It's not exactly an occupation and I don't plan on doing it for the rest of my life, but I work for phantazygrams. *(She walks to DR. GOLDIN and looks over her shoulder at what she's writing.)* It's one word—I always have to spell it for people—it's little P-H-A-N-T-A-Z … yes, Z, that's right … little Y… no space little G-R-A-M-S.

DR. GOLDIN. Got it. Thank you.

CANDY. You're welcome. You've got very neat handwriting—everything sits right on the lines.

DR. GOLDIN. Thank you.

CANDY. You're welcome. You should see mine—it's all over the place in every shape and size plus I doodle—endlessly—on anything and everything. *(Candy returns to her chair.)* Aaaanyway—back to phantazygrams—you know what it is—you call up and ask for a strippergram—one word—or a gorillagram—one word—or a bunnygram …

DR. GOLDIN. One word.

CANDY. Right—and then we deliver it to your husband or wife or boyfriend or girlfriend or whatever and, let me tell you, sometimes you'd be greatly surprised at the whatevers in LA.

DR. GOLDIN. *(indicating her costume)* So today …

CANDY. Uh-huh, I have a bunnygram gig right after this but I'm not a hooker if that's what you're thinking.

DR. GOLDIN. I'm sorry.

CANDY. It's just that when I tell people I work for phantazygrams, they sometimes jump to the conclusion that I'm a hooker and I'm not and I don't think I look like a hooker—do you think I look like a hooker?

DR. GOLDIN. It's not a good idea for a therapist to comment on …

CANDY. No—don't answer that because on some days I know I do look like a hooker but it's a fashion statement and that's not why I'm here anyway.

DR. GOLDIN. *(becoming professionally stern)* Before we proceed, I'd like to explain how I work and discuss fees.

CANDY. Oh, that's not really necessary.

DR. GOLDIN. *(with professional assurance)* Just to make certain there are no misconceptions as your therapy continues.

CANDY. My therapy isn't going to continue. And I'm paying for today's I-guess-you'd-call-it-a-session in cash.

DR. GOLDIN. Then I think there's been some misunderstanding. As I mentioned on the phone, my specialty is long-term therapy—not crisis intervention.

CANDY. Oh, this is going to take long-term therapy, for sure, there's no question about that as far as I can see and I can usually see pretty far when it comes to things like this.

(She goes to the coat rack and pulls money out of her shoulder bunnybag.)

DR. GOLDIN. Ms. Kane …

CANDY. Candy.

DR. GOLDIN. This is a bit irregular.

CANDY. If you only knew.

DR. GOLDIN. *(sternly)* In fact, it's highly irregular.

CANDY. Yes, it is, and, to be honest with you, I wasn't sure if I should pay you or if you should pay me.

DR. GOLDIN. *(standing)* Then I'm a little confused.

CANDY. I'm not surprised. *(handing DR. GOLDIN the money)* Here's a hundred and seventy-five dollars.

DR. GOLDIN. In ones?

CANDY. Tips. And you don't even have to let the IRS know about it—it's just between you and me—and, like I said, we don't have to talk about future sessions and actually, at first, I was thinking about just writing you a letter.

DR. GOLDIN. Therapy by mail?

CANDY. *(laughing politely)* Funny. *(then back to business)* But I couldn't do it. Too impersonal.

DR. GOLDIN. On the phone you said you had quite a serious problem.

CANDY. I know.

DR. GOLDIN. Have things improved since we talked?

CANDY. Oh, no, they're a lot worse—awful, terrible, catastrophic—that's how things are.

DR. GOLDIN. Can you tell me what's going on?

CANDY. Well, about a year ago I met someone. And, not surprisingly, I fell in love with him.

DR. GOLDIN. You say "not surprisingly" because …

CANDY. I may be certifiable but for me there's no such thing as dating or a one-night stand because for me going to bed with someone means we're married and, please, don't get me wrong, because I admit

I've been … *(She uses her fingers to make the quote/unquote gesture when she says the words* married, divorced, *and* aisle.*)* married and divorced hundreds of times but each time has been a walk down the aisle for me regardless of what it was for the guy.

DR. GOLDIN. You seem to be saying you develop instant, powerful attachments to the men you meet.

CANDY. *(raising her index finger to correct DR. GOLDIN)* Go to bed with.

DR. GOLDIN. You seem to be saying you develop instant, powerful attachments to the men you go to bed with.

CANDY. Exactly. Oh, I just found a Bazooka in my bunny pocket—do you mind if I chew while we talk?

DR. GOLDIN. No—by all means. So that's your problem.

CANDY. It's more that someone else has a problem that's the problem—here's my Bazooka fortune. *(She reads aloud the fortune from the Bazooka bubble gum wrapper:)* "'Today is tomorrow's yesterday." *(She gasps.)* Oh, my God! Can you believe that's my Bazooka fortune? This is freaky—really, really, really freaky.

DR. GOLDIN. *(with no humor about the proceedings)* And does this especially … freaky … *(DR. GOLDIN says the word* freaky *with a little discomfort since it's not her usual formal therapeutic terminology, with which she is more comfortable.)* … Bazooka fortune have something to do with your problem?

CANDY. *(suddenly with directness)* That's just it. It's not *my* problem. It's *your* problem. Your partner's having an affair.

DR. GOLDIN. *(shocked)* What did you say?

CANDY. Aimee's having an affair. Your Aimee. She's cheating on you.

(DR. GOLDIN tries valiantly to keep her professional composure, but she is shaken.)

DR. GOLDIN. I think perhaps there's been some mistake, Ms. Kane. *(attempting to hand the money back to her)* And please let me return your money to you and suggest we call an end to our … whatever it was.

CANDY. *(ignoring DR. GOLDIN's words, pushing the money back at her)* Please keep it because I feel so bad that I had to be the one to tell you and, oh, you should see yourself, I knew you'd get that look on your face, you know, the look that says you're trying to pretend that you don't believe that what the other person just said is true but you know in your heart of hearts that what the other person just said is true but you don't want the other person to think even for a second that you know it's true and you actually don't want to believe it's true yourself but you do. That look.

DR. GOLDIN. *(defensively)* How? How do you know? How do you know Aimee's having an affair? And who's she having it with?

CANDY. My boyfriend, Jeb, who also works at phantazygrams, which is where we met, and he does have a perfect body so I can't exactly blame her but I do.

DR. GOLDIN. We really cannot continue this discussion. It could cause devastating psychological trauma to … you. I strongly recommend that you seek professional counseling. *(CANDY doesn't move or say a word.)* Immediately. *(CANDY doesn't move or say a word.)* With someone else. *(CANDY doesn't move or say a word.)* Not here.

CANDY. *(centered and sure she's doing the right thing)* I'd want proof, too, because I really, actually, truly was on the Judge Judy show once and I lost though I don't think she considered all the facts of the case but I won't go into that now and, between you and me, I think the woman's a vindictive bitch and Dr. Laura can go take a flying leap, too, for my money after what she said to me on live radio. Okay, I'll give you proof if you insist.

DR. GOLDIN. I'm insisting you leave.

CANDY. Aimee's got a tiny, tiny, tiny little rose tattoo with a teeny, teeny, teeny little arrow through it—in a semi-private place.

DR. GOLDIN. *(fighting back a sinking feeling)* And … and, if she does, there are a hundred different ways you could know that without hearing it from your boyfriend.

CANDY. Oh, I didn't hear it from Jeb.

DR. GOLDIN. Well … then … maybe in your checkered career you were once … a tattooer's assistant … or … or … or ninety-nine other semi-private occupations like that!

CANDY. I wouldn't have accepted the tattoo evidence either. Sally Jesse Raphael is practically my mentor—she's tough but compassionate—and she always, always, always requires a scientifically administered lie detector test or DNA analysis. *(CANDY goes to the bunnybag again and pulls out a videotape. She hands it to DR. GOLDIN.)* Here.

DR. GOLDIN. And what, pray tell, is this? A large bunny dropping?

CANDY. Watch it.

DR. GOLDIN. I have no desire to watch to it. And if you leave it behind when you go on your hippity-hoppity way—I'll destroy it without even so much as a moment's hesitation. Do you understand? Do you hear what I'm saying?

CANDY. I hear you saying that you're feeling great pain.

DR. GOLDIN. *(as sarcastic as she ever gets and it's not much)* Thank you, Dr. Cottontail.

CANDY. *(sweetly, gently, calmly)* Like I said, I came here today not because I have a problem and need long-term therapy but because you have a problem and need long-term therapy and there's nothing to be ashamed of if you need to see someone about this and there's nothing to be ashamed of if you get angry and throw something and there's nothing to be ashamed of if you break down and sob until you hyperventilate. You have to go through the twelve steps of realizing that your lover is … is … *(She doesn't want to say the words again.)* Is. *(Pause)* Why is everything always twelve steps? Couldn't something terrible and awful and devastating to the body and soul heal in, say, three steps? Or maybe five at the most?

(DR. GOLDIN has listened deeply to CANDY's words. Then, without saying a word, like a woman going silently and bravely to the guillotine, DR. GOLDIN inserts the tape into a small television with a built-in VCR. We cannot see the screen—only the expressions on the faces of DR. GOLDIN and CANDY as they watch the tape.)

DR. GOLDIN. That isn't … that's not … *(moving closer to the TV)* That's Aimee. That's my … my. She's naked.

CANDY. And she is really, really, really pretty in that very sophisticated-anorexic-cocktail-party-at-a-hip-art-gallery-in-Malibu-drinking-Evian-kind-of way.

DR. GOLDIN. And there's a naked man there, too.

CANDY. That's Jeb.

DR. GOLDIN. I figured.

CANDY. Do you want to turn the audio on?

DR. GOLDIN. No thanks.

CANDY. Oh, my God, is that man handsome or what? He wants to break into the movies and I think he looks like one of the Baldwin brothers so I bet he ends up a big movie star someday because doesn't it seem like anyone who looks like a Baldwin brother makes it big? *(Pause)* I suddenly realize Aimee reminds me a little of Ingrid Bergman with that I'm-oh-so-fragile-I-might-break-into-into-a-thousand-little-shimmering pieces-of-crystal look she had in *Gaslight*, where Charles Boyer tried to drive her crazy. *(DR. GOLDIN goes into some form of shock as she watches the tape. She puts her hands over her eyes—as if she's watching a thriller. Then like a little girl, she peeks between her fingers—but even that is too much and she firmly clamps her hands over her eyes. CANDY pries DR. GOLDIN's hands away from her eyes, forcing her to watch. DR. GOLDIN's face is a funhouse mirror of contortion—stretching in and out of surprise, awe, anger, shame, and hurt at what she sees on the tape.)* Wow! Look at that! *(Pause)* See! There's the rose tattoo! *(Pause)* That's an unusual angle—don't you think? *(Pause)* You've got to admit Jeb's got a very good … cinematic eye.

(DR. GOLDIN turns off the TV.) (Pause)

DR. GOLDIN. I didn't know. *(Pause)*

CANDY. *(tenderly)* I knew you didn't know and I know what it's like not knowing until it all hits you smack in the face and I think it's better for you to know when they think you don't know. You know?

DR. GOLDIN. I didn't want to know. I didn't want to know.

CANDY. I am so sorry alot alot alot. But I came to help you. I really, actually, truly cross my heart and hope to die stick a thousand needles in my eye came to help you.

DR. GOLDIN. Help me? Do you realize I'll need crisis intervention counseling and long-term therapy for the rest of my life and possibly in the afterlife because of that tape?

CANDY. *(softly and sympathetically)* Yes.

DR. GOLDIN. *(crippled by the revelation)* I suppose you want me to confront Aimee so Jeb will be all yours again.

CANDY. No. Jeb doesn't love me—so why should I worry about holding onto him? I'm here because I couldn't bear standing by while you were getting hurt and not knowing it.

DR. GOLDIN. Not knowing you're getting hurt in love is the best kind of love there is.

CANDY. *(quietly)* No, it's not.

DR. GOLDIN. Why am I talking to a stranger who isn't even licensed in the state of California?

CANDY. I know I'm a stranger to you but you're not a stranger to me.

DR. GOLDIN. What in the world are you talking about?

CANDY. I've watched all of the Jeb and Aimee tapes.

DR. GOLDIN. Oh, my God! It's a series!

CANDY. *(off handedly)* Jeb likes having a multimedia record of all his exploits. *(softly)* Of course, at first, I thought I was all of his exploits. Then I stumbled on his archives. *(Pause)* Aaaanyway … on the tapes Aimee talks all about you.

DR. GOLDIN. She talks about me while they're making love?

CANDY. Oh, you know. A little here. A little there. And Jeb is pornographically curious about your lives together so he probes … as it were.

DR. GOLDIN. If only I could write myself a prescription for something.

CANDY. And, trust me, Dr. Goldin, it's crystal clear that Aimee adores you. She loves your independence of mind, your willingness to come to the rescue of the underdog at any time of day or night, your belief that you can make this a better world, your green eyes. She said all those things—one way or the other—on the tapes.

DR. GOLDIN. She did?

CANDY. Uh-huh. But it's also crystal clear that she feels … that she feels …

DR. GOLDIN. What? That she feels what?

CANDY. Like first runner-up in the Miss America Contest.

DR. GOLDIN. You mean …

CANDY. Aimee thinks that, in your eyes, your career, your seriousness of purpose, your concern about all the underdogs that come your way are the winner; she thinks that, in your eyes, they're Miss America. She thinks she only comes in a distant second. Isn't the Miss America pageant a travesty? Of course, I watch it every year. Who doesn't? But I always turn it off when they finally announce Miss America because I can't stand looking at the faces of the first, second, third, and, oh, how pathetic, the fourth runner-up as they try not to look devastated. So I understand how Aimee feels.

DR. GOLDIN. She feels second in my life?

CANDY. Uh-huh.

DR. GOLDIN. But that's not the way it is in my … in my …

CANDY. I wish you could say the word. It would be an important breakthrough.

(DR. GOLDIN staggers a bit with emotion and falls back into the patient's chair.)

DR. GOLDIN. In my … heart …

CANDY. Oh, thank God! You said it. There's hope.

DR. GOLDIN. For what?

CANDY. Here's why I came …

DR. GOLDIN. Yes—why did you come?

CANDY. To help you save your marriage—if you want.

DR. GOLDIN. How?

CANDY. See, I was thinking, at first, about writing Sally Jesse Raphael and trying to interest her in a show on the tragedy of bisexual extramarital dalliances and getting her to invite you and me and Aimee and Jeb on to tell our story. But then I turned on the TV one day and what do I see on Sally Jesse Raphael but a show on the tragedy of bisexual extramarital dalliances so I said forget it.

DR. GOLDIN. Good. I'm glad that's not the reason you're here. Because I may be certifiable, but I'm not going on national television and tell everybody and their extended, dysfunctional families that I'm a psychiatrist of a certain sexual persuasion whose lover is cheating on her with a gorillagram!

CANDY. You don't have to because I realized that there's a much easier and more effective way to win back Aimee.

DR. GOLDIN. I'm all ears.

CANDY. My analyst says that …

DR. GOLDIN. Oh, my God! You have an analyst? Do I know him or her? Have you mentioned names and addresses?

CANDY. Actually it's my friend Jade who works at phantazygrams and she's not really licensed or anything but she's a very intuitive herbalist who does therapy with animals.

DR. GOLDIN. Well, then you're in good hands.

CANDY. *(laughing politely)* Funny. *(then back to business)* Aaaaanyway Jade's analysis of Jeb is that he's an extreme narcissist with sexual performance issues and her analysis of Aimee is that she's adrift on an existential sea, experimenting with anybody who climbs aboard her dingy—because she feels like a blank, a void, a nobody … to you … whom she loves most in the world.

DR. GOLDIN. Wow! Jade's good. Is she taking any new patients?

CANDY. So here's my idea—we're going to make our own video and I'll make sure it falls into Jeb's and Aimee's hands.

DR. GOLDIN. A video?

CANDY. Telling Aimee what you really feel about her.

DR. GOLDIN. But shouldn't I just tell her in person?

CANDY. It's like getting an anonymous gift. It's so much more powerful if someone thinks they're overhearing what wasn't meant for them to hear.

DR. GOLDIN. Candy, I don't know if that'll work.

CANDY. Dr. Goldin …

DR. GOLDIN. Jane …

CANDY. Jane, this is LA. Land of hundreds of disgruntled ex-Disney employees and the one place on Earth where everything is more convincing on film. Didn't it make a difference when I showed you the video today?

DR. GOLDIN. Yes … yes, it did.

CANDY. Okay, now here's the idea. It's as simple as telling the truth.

DR. GOLDIN. I always warn my patients that there's nothing simple about telling the truth.

CANDY. I'll say I got furious when I stumbled on the tapes with Jeb and Aimee and demanded that you meet me at Jeb's so that, one, I could show you the incriminating tapes and, two, we could hash things out. I'll also admit that, unbeknownst to you, I videotaped our encounter as proof to them that the jig is up. But Aimee will see your true colors shining through and she'll shove Jeb out of that dingy quicker than you can say "Tallulah Bankhead in *Lifeboat*." And, I predict—she'll come running back to you heart and soul just like in the movies.

DR. GOLDIN. I don't know. I don't think I could pull it off.

CANDY. Wait till you read my script.

(She goes to her bunnybag and pulls out two scripts, handing one to DR. GOLDIN.)

DR. GOLDIN. Script?

CANDY. *(quickly skimming to find the part of the script she wants to rehearse)* Skip to … page … three … halfway down the page. Now remember—at this point we'll be, for all intents and purposes, two angry women fighting for our men … our women … our man and woman.

DR. GOLDIN. I'll try.

CANDY. Let's just run a few lines to get the feel. *(Suddenly noticing something about DR. GOLDIN.)* Oh, my gosh.

DR. GOLDIN. What's wrong?

CANDY. You're going to need a makeover.

DR. GOLDIN. A makeover?

CANDY. For starters, take off that suit jacket. You look like Michael Eisner. *(DR. GOLDIN obeys—now that she is completely under CANDY's spell.)* Good. Now unbutton the top buttons on your blouse. *(DR. GOLDIN is embarrassed and hesitates.)* Come on, Jane. Remember—this is all in the name of love. *(DR. GOLDIN unbuttons several buttons and suddenly in her pale peach blouse with cleavage, her transformation begins.)* Good. Now the hair. Please set your hair free. It's giving me a headache just looking at it. *(DR. GOLDIN takes a pin or two out of her hair, shakes her hair free, and looks smashing.)* You won't believe what's happening to you. You're just like Kim Novak in *Vertigo* when Jimmy Stewart redoes her. Now take off your glasses.

DR. GOLDIN. I can't see without them.

CANDY. Well, Aimee can. *(DR. GOLDIN takes off her glasses.)* Oh, Jane, look at yourself! *(DR. GOLDIN goes to a mirror near the door.)*

DR. GOLDIN. Can I put on my glasses?

CANDY. No.

DR. GOLDIN. *(with her nose practically up against the mirror)* Wow.

CANDY. Wow is right. Okay back to the script.

DR. GOLDIN. Can I wear my glasses?

CANDY. For rehearsals only. For the filming—no.

DR. GOLDIN. Fair enough.

CANDY. *(pointing to a place in the script)* Okay. Let's start here. My line is first. *(reading from the script)* "So I suppose you don't care about all this. I suppose you and your ... friend ... have some sort of arrangement. Anything goes with you people—right? Well, don't you have anything to say?" *(DR. GOLDIN gazes at CANDY with affectionate awe.) (pointing to the script)* Now you say your big speech. It starts right here.

DR. GOLDIN. *(reading from the script—stiffly)* "At first, when you told me—and then showed me—that my Aimee was having an affair, I couldn't believe it. I refused to believe it."

CANDY. *(giving her notes)* A little looser. A little more emotion. Remember—I've just sprung some shocking news on you.

DR. GOLDIN. Oh, okay. Can we start over?

CANDY. Sure. *(reading from the script)* "Well, don't you have anything to say?"

DR. GOLDIN. *(reading from the script—getting better)* "At first, when you told me—and then showed me—that my Aimee was having an affair, I couldn't believe it. I refused to believe it."

CANDY. Good. Stay nice and loose like that.

DR. GOLDIN. *(reading from the script—improving word by word)* "Of course, I know how lovely she is. How unique she is. How desirable she is to so many people. And I suppose I always knew something like this might happen someday and always wondered what I'd feel if it did."

CANDY. That's it! Now you're beginning to make me feel your sincerity, your passion, your sense of loss.

DR. GOLDIN. *(suddenly seeing what a dear person CANDY is under her bunny fur)* You know, Candy, this is awfully nice of you to try to help.

CANDY. It's the least I could do, Jane.

DR. GOLDIN. Should I go on?

CANDY. Yes. Start from the beginning.

(In the following speech, DR. GOLDIN reveals all her tenderness of feeling toward Aimee in a natural, easy, moving way. This is an Oscar caliber performance.)

DR. GOLDIN. *(reading from the script)* "At first, when you told me—and then showed me—that my Aimee was having an affair, I couldn't believe it. I refused to believe it. Of course, I know how lovely she is. How unique she is. How desirable she is to so many people. And I suppose I always knew something like this might happen someday and always wondered what I'd feel if it did. And now I know. Now I know how I feel." *(The script falls to DR. GOLDIN's side. She takes off her glasses and is no longer reading from the script. The following comes straight from, yes, her heart.)* I feel as if I'm falling through space. I feel as if nothing is real. I feel as if everything around me—this room, this street, this Earth are nothing but a shabby set built by some cruel god as some cruel trick. Without the one I love, without Aimee, there is no world for me. There is no world at all.

(DR. GOLDIN's stands motionless, eyes gleaming with passion. CANDY cries softly at DR. GOLDIN's performance.)

CANDY. *(quietly)* No one has ever loved me like that.

DR. GOLDIN. *(quietly)* Someone will.

CANDY. *(needing to believe)* You think?

DR. GOLDIN. I know.

CANDY. Oh, I hope so—alot alot alot.

DR. GOLDIN. Do you think it will work with Aimee?

CANDY. Do I think it will work with Aimee? It would work in every movie theater in America.

DR. GOLDIN. *(with a smile)* So—was that a take?

CANDY. *(drying her tears, with a laugh)* Yes, Jane Goldin, star of stage, screen, and home video—that was a take.

BLACKOUT

"They Can't Take That Away From Me"

(SCENE:The Monterey, California, backyard of the exquisite and expensive home of DR. KIT MARCH and DR. KEENE WINFIELD, a married couple whom we first met when they were single in "I'll Take Manhattan" in Act One. A magnificently sculpted redwood deck looks out on a beautiful lawn running down to a cliff and the Pacific Ocean beyond.

TIME:Just before sunset on a midsummer's evening.

AT RISE, KEENE, looking tanned and fit and dressed in exquisite and expensive designer-label summer wear, is sitting in a deck chair, staring pensively out across the lawn.

A bottle of champagne is cooling on ice and four champagne glasses sit expectantly on a low table.

KIT, looking tanned and fit and dressed in exquisite and expensive designer-label summer wear, enters waving a check.

In the following exchanges between KIT and KEENE, there is a formality that seems at odds with the celebratory nature of what they are saying to each other.)

KIT. Pop the cork!

KEENE. Good news?

KIT. I finally got around to the mail, and—what should I discover?—but an envelope, from whatever conglomerate it is that owns our publisher at the moment, containing a nice, chubby little royalty check!

(KIT waves the check in front of KEENE teasingly, finally letting him read the amount.)

KEENE. Definitely nice and definitely chubby. You're right—this does call for a pop!

(He pops the champagne bottle open.)

KIT. I love that sound. *(KEENE pours the bubbly into two glasses.)* I'd say a toast is in order—what do you think?
KEENE. It's a must.
KIT. May I?
KEENE. Be my guest.

(They raise their glasses.)

KIT. Here's to *The Cracker Jack Prize Paradigm* …
KEENE. Colon: *One Life, Many Loves.*
KIT. *(with a tone of competition)* By *March* and Winfield.
KEENE. *(with a matching tone of competition)* By *Winfield* and March.
KIT. Still going strong at twenty-six weeks on the *New York Times* nonfiction bestseller list.
KEENE. Cheers!
KIT. Cheers!

(They touch glasses and take a sip of champagne.)

KEENE. And to think: We gave birth to a self-help book that's self-helping—who knows?—maybe hundreds of thousands of people!
KIT. In seventeen different languages—including Flemish.
KEENE. It's …
KIT. Exhilarating.
KEENE. And a little scary.
KIT. Scary?
KEENE. Think about it. People all over the world are taking our advice.
KIT. Well, it's good advice. Why shouldn't they take it?

KEENE. I don't know. It just seems that Flemland might have something more important on its mind than romantic relationships.

KIT. Like what?

KEENE. Flem? *(Pause)* Or something.

KIT. What could possibly be more important than romantic relationships? They're all we've got. They're the only thing that distinguishes us from the rest of the animal kingdom.

KEENE. Hold it right there. A blue bower male flies far and wide hunting for fuzz and thingamajigs that are blue—and only blue—to present to his would-be mate. I'd call that romance.

KIT. Do they send funny valentines? Do they take wedding videos?

KEENE. Do they file petitions for divorce? No. No, they don't. *(Pause). (Now the reason for the formality between KIT and KEENE is becoming clear.)* And, by the way, I want to thank you for being so honest this morning about … things.

KIT. Your openness made it possible. And you agreed …

KEENE. Of course. It's been obvious to me for some time now.

KIT. Who could ever have imagined that our chance meeting two years ago in Dr. Freeman's office in Gramercy Park would have led us to the altar in Connecticut …

KEENE. Then to our couples' practice here in Monterey …

KIT. And now down the trail of … well … *(raising her glass)* Happy trails, Keene.

KEENE. *(raising his glass)* Happy trails, Kit. *(They touch glasses and take a sip of champagne.)* Who knows? If I'd been able to keep my appointment with Dr. Freeman, I might be married Caroline right this minute.

KIT. And you may yet—one life, many loves.

KEENE. And Angelo may still play a role in your life again. Or Barry.

KIT. Not unless they split up.

KEENE. That was a surprise—wasn't it? And they still seem so awfully happy.

KIT. *(with an edge)* Yes—they still seem so awfully happy. *(Pause)* What do think, Keene? This weekend … will we mention our … decision?

KEENE. Let's just allow the energy to flow through us and speak for itself.

KIT. Yes, of course, how many times have we counseled couples to do that very thing?

KEENE. We'll probably want to make this our last couple-on-couple weekend workshop here at the house.

KIT. I agree. It should be our last. And I think we're lucky to be working with the Moores. Such a nice, young couple—to be ending our practice with.

KEENE. I liked them from our very first interview.

KIT. Dinah appears to be a little more on edge than Teddy today—but there's always one in a couple who seems to feel the problems more deeply.

KEENE. I think that's right. I only hope we can help them in some way. *(KEENE spots TEDDY and DINAH stepping onto the upper deck. He beckons to them, smiles, and welcomes them brightly.)* And here they are now. *(TEDDY MOORE enters jauntily with DINAH, his wife, who is holding his hand but who is trailing a little behind, feeling already unhinged about the weekend. They are wearing casual summer clothes, of a much less expensive kind than the doctors. KEENE goes to them as they come down the steps to the lower deck and shakes their hands warmly. TEDDY is instantly likeable, with a friendly, easy, straightforward manner that is radiantly irresistible. DINAH seems to have an almost visible storm cloud of emotion around her in her hesitancy and self-consciousness. Many of the things DINAH says end with an invisible question mark of doubt.)* Well, you two look much more relaxed. Is your room comfortable?

TEDDY. *(with gusto)* Absolutely.

DINAH. *(sounding as if she's asking a question)* Absolutely.

KEENE. *(hands them glasses he has filled with champagne)* Excellent. Then let's raise our glasses to a weekend of joyful discovery. *(The four raise their glasses and take a sip of champagne. DINAH chokes. TEDDY pats her lovingly on the back until she recovers.)* Why don't we sit and enjoy the sunset. *(Each of the four finds a comfortable place to sit.)*

TEDDY. The sky is magnificent tonight. Isn't it, honey?

(When DINAH leans back in her chaise longue, it slides flat so she is lying on her back, tenuously holding onto her champagne glass, looking straight up at the sky.)

DINAH. Magnificent, sweetheart.

(KEENE adjusts DINAH's chaise longue and helps make her comfortable.)

KEENE. There we go. *(realizing that the only way to break the ice is to start to work)* Teddy, Dinah …

DINAH. *(nervously)* Yes?

KEENE. *(smiling warmly)* As you know, our work is exclusively with couples …

TEDDY. Well, then I think we qualify—don't we, Dinah?

DINAH. *(ending with another question mark)* Yes.

KEENE. And beginning this very moment and ending on Sunday afternoon, the weekend is for the two of you to explore your relationship while we serve as your emotional Sherpa guides.

TEDDY. It sounds wonderful. We've really been looking forward to this. When we found your book and discovered you do workshops—we felt as if fate were leading us to you.

KEENE. We have only three simple guidelines for the weekend. Simple—and yet the most challenging you'll ever face in your life together.

(DINAH chugalugs her glass of champagne. Everyone notices without judgment, and KEENE simply refills the glass. They all watch, expecting her to chugalug once more. But this time DINAH takes only a tiny sip.)

KIT. One: Communicate. Say what you're thinking and feeling. Two: Concentrate. Stay in the moment. Don't allow yourself to escape what is happening by thinking about the past or the future. And Three: Elevate. Honor your inner child. If you begin to feel angry or hurt or threatened, express the emotion but express it creatively. Dance, blow bubbles in your champagne, use one of the instruments in this bench … *(KIT opens the lid to a bench that has a storage compartment.)* We have a drum, a triangle, sand blocks, and so on. But—use no words!—until you can bring the golden circle of communication back to rule one and just begin anew with a calm heart.

TEDDY. *(thrilled)* Wow! It sounds great! Doesn't it, Dinah?

DINAH. Uh-huh.

KEENE. We've abbreviated the steps into a kind of mantra—so we can all easily remind ourselves to stay squarely on the path of enlightenment.

KIT. One—Communicate. Two—Concentrate. Three—Elevate.

KEENE. Let's all say it together.

(DINAH lags a hesitant beat behind as the others chant the mantra.)

ALL. One—Communicate. Two—Concentrate. Three—Elevate.

KEENE. Good! Let me also say from the start: Kit and I have no agenda—only the hope that, in this time and space, the two of you will be able to see each other and your issues with more understanding and acceptance. What happens may lead to a resolution of your issues and the flourishing of your relationship. Or, as we discussed extensively in our sessions online and on the phone, with unresolvable issues—your individual paths of growth may diverge and lead in separate directions.

(DINAH begins softly crying.)

KIT. Dinah, remember number three: Elevate. Honor your inner child creatively. *(DINAH is at a loss in this therapeutic setting but wants to make the weekend work for the sake of her marriage. So without much enthusiasm, she picks up an elegant glass straw from the table and blows bubbles in her champagne glass. Finally, she stops.)* That's the spirit. Didn't it feel good?

DINAH. *(sounding as if she's asking a question)* Uh-huh.

(DINAH chugalugs the contents of her champagne glass again. KEENE obligingly refills her glass.)

KEENE. Alright—the mantra is in place—let the Zen begin.

KIT. Who's going to start?

DINAH. *(hesitantly)* Should I, Teddy?

KIT. Who's going to start?

TEDDY. *(tenderly)* We agreed you would.

DINAH. Teddy and I have been married now for three and a half years. *(beaming at TEDDY in happy remembrance)* We met at Starbucks. Teddy was sitting at a table by himself, with his laptop, working on a screenplay.

TEDDY. *(good-humoredly)* Everybody at Starbucks in California has a laptop and is working on a screenplay.

DINAH. The only chair that wasn't taken was the one at his table so I asked if I could sit there. And we just started talking over our nonfat decaffeinated lattes.

TEDDY. *(warmly)* Love at first nonfat decaffeinated sip.

DINAH. *(becoming unglued when she says the words* "all this"*)* It was. And I'd call ours a perfect marriage until … all this … started happening.

(DINAH, goes to the bench, opens the lid, picks up a triangle, and dings it madly. The other three honor her expression of emotion and pause in their conversation until she is done and places the triangle back in the bench.)

KEENE. Excellent, Dinah.

KIT. Can you tell us what "all this" is and when it started happening?

TEDDY. *(tenderly)* May I, Dinah?

DINAH. *(with a quaver in her voice)* Please, honey.

TEDDY. *(eagerly and charmingly)* I think it would be fair to say that Dinah is concerned about me, which, of course, makes her concerned about us as a couple. Right, sweetheart?

DINAH. *(with a quaver in her voice, trying to stay in control)* Yes.

TEDDY. Dinah's parents are concerned, too. We borrowed the money for the workshop from them—otherwise we could never have afforded it ourselves. As you know, I teach high school English and Dinah's a social worker.

DINAH. Mom and Dad love Teddy and have been very supportive.

TEDDY. I guess, when all is said and done, it boils down to this: Dinah wants things to be the way they were … before.

KIT. Before what?

(TEDDY looks lovingly at DINAH and can barely say the words he knows will hurt her.)

TEDDY. Before she found out about me. I've known about myself … about my true nature … for a while now. And I've been able to hide my feelings, keep them buried. But then several months ago, I found I just couldn't betray my true self for one more minute.

(DINAH goes to the bench, opens the lid, pulls out a kazoo, and kazoos madly. The other three honor her expression of emotion and pause in their conversation until she is done and places the kazoo back in the bench.)

KEENE. Good, Dinah.

KIT. So, Teddy, you were saying … you told Dinah about yourself…

TEDDY. Well, actually—she caught me in the act.

KIT. Was this at home?

TEDDY. Yes.

KIT. In the bed you share?

TEDDY. No, in the backyard. I think it might not have been so devastating for Dinah if there hadn't been so many witnesses.

KIT. People saw what you were doing?

TEDDY. And heard—everything. In fact, it was probably the noise that first attracted their attention.

KIT. Teddy—painful though this may be for Dinah and you—can you please tell us the exact nature of the act you were performing in the backyard and with whom you were performing it?

TEDDY. I was doing it alone.

KIT. Doing what?

TEDDY. Howling at the moon.

KIT. So what you're saying is that … Dinah found you in the backyard … alone … howling at the moon.

TEDDY. Uh-huh.

KEENE. Dinah, what were your feelings when you found Teddy howling at the moon?

DINAH. At first I thought he was joking and I laughed.

TEDDY. You haven't heard it yet—but Dinah has the sweetest laugh in the world.

DINAH. Then the neighborhood dogs started joining in. And, one after the other, all the neighbors came out to see what was going on. I begged Teddy to stop.

TEDDY. But I couldn't.

KIT. Why not?

DINAH. I asked the same question. Didn't I, Teddy?

TEDDY. You did—and I truly didn't know why at the time. Only days after my first howling did I begin to get an inkling of what it was all about.

KIT. *(extremely curious)* And what *is* it all about?

TEDDY. I think it has something to do with ... a longing to go home.

KIT. Yes—in your application and interviews you mentioned that moving back home had become a matter of controversy between the two of you. Where is home, Teddy?

TEDDY. I don't know exactly. Most likely somewhere beyond the Milky Way. I only know I'm not from Earth.

(KIT and KEENE exchange a glance as if to say, "They didn't tell us everything in their interviews.")

DINAH. This never came up in any way before we were married.

TEDDY. Honey, I didn't know.

(In the course of the preceding scene, the sky has gone from a huge azure canvas with a horizon of creamy pink and yellow ribbons to an azure sky with a ribbon of crimson at the horizon. Now the canvas darkens to a deep blue with a few wisps of white cloud. KEENE picks up a remote control and turns on the deck lights, bringing them up gently, creating a romantic mood.)

KIT. Teddy, what makes you think your need to howl has anything to do with what you call your "longing to go home"?

TEDDY. At first, I didn't realize there was any connection. But the more I've given over to my howl, the more I see home. Still only in lightning moments. In flickers and flashes. But I see it.

KIT. And what do you see in those lightning moments?

TEDDY. I suppose you think I'm going to describe some idyllic sci-fi Utopia—with magenta skies and crystal rivers and wild ponies that speak with tongues of flame …

KIT. We're honestly trying not to make any assumptions at all—right, Keene?

KEENE. *(stunned at the turn of events)* I couldn't make an assumption if I tried.

TEDDY. Good. Because that's not what it's like.

KIT. What *is* it like?

TEDDY. Well, adding up all the puzzle pieces that go flying through my brain, I guess I'd have to say something like Iowa with Mozart.

KIT. Can you explain?

TEDDY. It's flat, I think, and something green grows in rows and rows …

KIT. And the Mozart?

TEDDY. It seems that when the seasons change—there are twelve altogether—the nearby planets move into harmonious alignment … and make the most delicate music … that calms and soothes the spirits of everyone … the sweetest, gentlest, most intoxicating music you can imagine … like Mozart. *(KIT and DINAH appear charmed by TEDDY's words. KEENE is stunned.)* I don't want you to get the wrong impression. It's not paradise—everyone works and works hard. But there's no threatening ladder of success to climb up or fall down because no one feels demeaned or diminished or disappointed by what they do for a living. Or in competition with anybody else for anything. And, oh! Oh! The best part is—it's a place where you can say anything that's in your heart without offending or hurting someone. Words there only heal.

KIT. And, by contrast, you believe that here—in this world—you can't say what's in your heart.

TEDDY. *(with a tender knowing)* Let's say that here on Earth, words fail us and we fail words—more than words can say. (*PAUSE. Then to KIT.)* Don't you agree?

KIT. *(trying to avoid answering his question)* Well … you know … it doesn't matter whether I agree or not. This weekend is about you and Dinah and if and how the two of you do or do not agree.

TEDDY. There! That's what I mean!

KIT. What? What's what you mean?

TEDDY. I ask if you think we can ever say what's in our hearts and you throw up a smoke screen to avoid telling me what's in yours.

KEENE. *(an unedited personal, not professional response)* Kit, Teddy's right. You didn't answer his question.

(KIT throws KEENE a glance of annoyance.)

KIT. Well, then, yes, I think we can say what's in our heart … to others … in this world.

TEDDY. Prove it!

KIT. What proof would satisfy you?

TEDDY. Tell me what's going on in your heart—right this minute!

KIT. There are accepted rules of behavior for a doctor working with patients … clients.

TEDDY. And a doctor can't share her personal feelings—right?

KIT. Right.

TEDDY. Poor Earth! What a sad, sad planet.

KIT. But this isn't the world. Maybe a doctor and client can't talk heart-to-heart—but a husband and wife can.

TEDDY. Can you and your husband?

KIT. *(glancing at KEENE for support)* We're very open with each other.

TEDDY. Can you say anything and everything?

KIT. *(glancing again at KEENE for support)* As I said—we're very open with each other. *(PAUSE. KIT glances a third time at KEENE for support.)*

KEENE. *(finally, rallying poorly)* Yes—we're very open with each other.

TEDDY. *(with passion)* It's not the same. Don't try and trick me with words. This is too important. I want to know! Is there ever a moment when two people from this world can let the masks fall? Is there ever a second of seeing that isn't distorted by some secret insecurity or sense of self-importance? Some hidden shame or fear or longing or regret? Is there? Is there?

KIT. *(weakly)* Well …

TEDDY. Doesn't it become unbearable sometimes? The longing to say what's in your heart, the longing to hear what's in someone else's? Don't you find yourself thinking about it at the oddest times? When the doctor's examining your ears ... or you're standing next to a stranger waiting in line for the bus ... or you're looking across the table at someone you've looked across the table at a thousand times before? Doesn't the longing tear at you like a wild animal? Don't you want to cry out: "Let's see each other as we really are! For God's sake—let's love each other as we really are!"

(KIT suddenly stands and turns her back to the three. She raises a hand with a tissue to her eyes, bending her head.)

KEENE. Kit, are you alright?

KIT. Yes, it's just my contact acting up. *(Pause)*

TEDDY. *(kindly, to KIT)* I hear you saying that you're feeling great pain.

KIT. *(lying, turning back to the group, trying to recover her professional composure, crisply)* I am—in my eye.

TEDDY. Anyway ... that's why I want to go home. That's why the longing is so great. And when I see the moon ... *(A pale lemon yellow moon, achingly beautiful, slips out from behind a wisp of cloud. TEDDY does not at first see the moon, but the other three do. DINAH covers her mouth with her hand as if to stop herself from screaming.)* ... it comes over me. A longing ... of indescribable enormity ... and I have to howl—or go crazy! *(TEDDY senses the tension in the air and realizes that something of which he is not aware must be happening. DINAH's skyward gaze alerts him, and he spins around looking for what he guesses the other three have seen.) (ecstatic and radiant in his ecstasy)* See! See how beautiful it is! *(KIT, KEENE, and DINAH are transfixed in wonder at TEDDY'S words and behavior.)* Don't you feel it? Don't you feel the power of it? Doesn't it call out to you?

(TEDDY's clothes seem to melt away from him, and he stands resplendent, before the other three, in a bikini bathing suit that seems almost not to be there. He is bathed in moonlight, his arms outspread to the universe, inviting wonder into his soul. The moon

has grown brighter and somehow more magical. Suddenly and surprisingly, DINAH stands. She chugalugs her glass of champagne yet again. At first, it isn't clear how she is reacting to TEDDY or what she is going to do. Then all hesitancy and self-consciousness fall away from her.)

DINAH. Yes! Yes! Yes! Yes, I do—my darling one! Teddy's made me feel something I've never felt before in my entire life. A freedom … *(DINAH whirls slowly and gracefully around the deck.)* To look at who I am …

(DINAH's clothes seem to melt away from her, and she stands resplendent, beside TEDDY, in a bikini bathing suit that seems almost not to be there. She is bathed in moonlight, her arms outspread to the universe, inviting wonder into her soul.)

TEDDY. And when I howl at the moon, it begins in a place of deep, sad longing …

DINAH. To know who I am …

TEDDY. Then it takes me to a place of wild, tender ecstasy …

DINAH. To be who I am …

TEDDY. Where I can embrace everything, everything I know I am!

DINAH. To love who I am …

TEDDY. Without sham. Without pretense. Only with love. *(TEDDY and DINAH fall on their knees and begin howling at the moon with a deep, sad longing that becomes a wild, tender, ecstatic embrace of their souls. TEDDY and DINAH complete their communion, slump momentarily as if from exhaustion, compose themselves, stand, and return quietly to their chairs. KIT and KEENE haven't moved an inch.) (sweetly, quietly)* Longing to go home … that's why I howl.

KEENE. *(stunned)* Ah.

KIT. *(astonished by TEDDY's nearly naked joyfulness)* Oh!

DINAH. *(sweetly, quietly)* And longing to follow Teddy … that's why I howl.

KEENE. *(stunned)* Ah.

KIT. *(astonished by DINAH's nearly naked joyfulness)* Oh!

(TEDDY and DINAH smile radiantly.)

KIT. *(confused—trying to understand)* Then … then … then … Keene, step in here at any time …

KEENE. Then, Dinah, you *want* to follow Teddy to his home … planet—right?

DINAH. Who wouldn't want to?

KIT. *(back in control of her own thoughts)* So what's the problem? What's the issue?

DINAH. *(sweetly, with terrible pain)* What if someday they … Teddy's people … come and take him back … take him away from me … and leave me all alone? What would I do?

KEENE. But, Teddy, couldn't you take Dinah with you?

TEDDY. *(shaking his head sadly)* There's no telling.

DINAH. Since Teddy found your book and made me read it, he's begged me to accept your idea of "one life, many loves." And to leave him—now! To find another love. To avoid a lifetime of dread at the possibility of losing him … at any moment … without a second's warning. *(with strong emotion)* But I can't. I can't accept the idea of having a tumbling heart forever.

KEENE. A tumbling heart?

DINAH. I have a quilt my grandmother made, in a pattern called Tumbling Hearts. And when you look at it, all the hearts—in every color and pattern imaginable—seem to be tumbling, tumbling, endlessly tumbling. *(with great passion)* And I can't bear the thought of giving up Teddy. Of having him torn away from me. Of living without the one person who makes me feel so completely alive. Of having a heart tumbling, tumbling, endlessly tumbling for a lifetime. I'd rather die!

(DINAH's words have struck everyone dumb.)

KEENE. *(trying to stabilize the situation)* Well, well, well. Dinah, Teddy, orientation is coming to an end, and I think we've zeroed in on your issue. *(looking at his watch)* So I think this would be a good time for us to break. We'll have dinner in half an hour—Anna will be serving her irresistible grilled salmon with picante sauce. And we'll conduct our after-dinner session in the hot tub, which ... *(smiling and gesturing toward their bathing suits)* ... you're all ready for. But before we close, let me just leave us all with the reminder that love is never immutable. It's ever-changing. The greatest of poets have whispered that truth in our ears throughout the ages. Shakespeare—as you, no doubt, know, Teddy—wrote a play, a comedy, called *Love's Labours Lost.* *(KEENE says the following in an effort to plant the seed for what he assumes will be DINAH's fate.)* We mention it in our book. It's always served as a touchstone for us, a cue to remember to accept our losses—and move on. This weekend, Dinah, let's explore how you might not only survive without Teddy—but maybe even thrive without him. And remember they ... Teddy's people ... can't take away from you all that the two of you have shared. You'll always have those memories. *(Pause)* How does that sound as a way for us to proceed?

(DINAH is feeling great stress. She opens the lid to the bench and pulls out a party whistle that, when blown, sends out a paper tongue. She's so overcome with emotion that she can hardly get the paper tongue half way out before it rolls pathetically back up again, making almost no whistling sound at all. Looking at KEENE and then at TEDDY, she throws down the whistle and runs off— terrified by KEENE's words. Perhaps from DINAH's deep emotions, KIT turns quietly away from TEDDY and KEENE. She raises a tissue to her eyes again. TEDDY smiles a quizzically beguiling smile at KEENE as if to say, "This is why we're here." KEENE nods in understanding. TEDDY begins to follow DINAH, then turns back.)

TEDDY. I didn't want to mention this while Dinah was here, but did you know some scholars believe Shakespeare wrote several plays that are lost to us?

KEENE. Oh?

TEDDY. Uh-huh—and one was a sequel ... called *Love's Labours Won.*

(KEENE starts to answer but no words come out of his mouth. TEDDY smiles his radiant smile and hurries after DINAH. KEENE is

momentarily lost in thought and then remembers KIT. He looks toward her and sees that she has turned away.)

KEENE. Kit, what's wrong? What is it?

KIT. *(turning to face him)* They're disturbed! They're delusional! They're demented! They're crazy people!

KEENE. *(gently)* Kit, this is California.

KIT. Keene, they think he's from somewhere beyond the Milky Way! *(KIT picks up the party whistle DINAH has tossed down and blows and blows and blows—flaring the paper tongue all the way out and all the way back, again and again and again.) (quietly)* And so am I.

KEENE. Oh, my God! You think you're from somewhere beyond the Milky Way, too?

KIT. No—I think I'm just a crazy person … from Manhattan. *(Pause)* Keene, this morning when I asked you for a divorce …

KEENE. *(with love)* Don't worry. I've already thought it over. We don't even have to negotiate it. You can have the Chagall.

KIT. Keene, this morning when I asked you for a divorce, I didn't want a divorce. I didn't want you to say, "Yes, one life—many loves." I wanted you say, "Never in a million years! I'll tie us both to subway tracks. I'll throw us both off the Empire State Building. I'll hire someone from Long Island for a double hit. But I'll never! never! never! agree to a divorce! One life—one love!" *(The following exchanges between KIT and KEENE are quiet, tender, and real.)* That's what I wanted you to say.

KEENE. I thought you were testing me, Kit—about the principles in our book. I thought you wanted me to be strong and sure and full of our book's convictions. Like all those people in Flemland.

KIT. No. Being married to you and loving you as I've come to do has made me see our book is . . . all baloney.

KEENE. Really?

KIT. Really. This morning all I wanted was for you to be weak and uncertain and riddled with doubt about everything—except wanting me. Instead you agreed—without a moment's hesitation! I've been guessing that's what your silence has been about.

KEENE. My silence? I talk all the time.

KIT. For our entire marriage, you've barely spoken one intimate word to me. And I've wanted to cry out to you over your *Nabisco Shredded Wheat*—"Tell me what you're thinking! Tell me what you're feeling! Tell me what's in your heart! I'm here! I'm here! I'm listening!" *(Pause)* I've been on the phone for hours about it with Dr. Freeman! *(KIT turns away from KEENE, who is mostly stunned.) (Pause) (sweetly)* Well—aren't you going to say something? Please aren't you going to say something?

KEENE. What did Dr. Freeman say?

KIT. "Talk to him."

KEENE. Funny. That's what he said to me.

KIT. You've been on the phone with Dr. Freeman?

KEENE. Yes.

KIT. Dr. Louis Freeman?

KEENE. Yes.

KIT. Dr. Louis J. Freeman?

KEENE. Yes!

KIT. What did he say?

KEENE. "Talk to her."

KIT. Why didn't you?

KEENE. Because … because you've always been so perfect …

KIT. *(disbelieving—it's not her perception of herself)* Me? Perfect?

KEENE. Uh-huh. It's always seemed so much easier for me to talk to someone who's just a little bit of a mess. Maybe that's why I went into psychiatry.

KIT. Oh, Keene. If only I'd known—I could have been a mess for you so easily. I was afraid you wouldn't love me if I ever fell to pieces in front of you.

KEENE. And maybe, too, because we've always been so … competitive.

KIT. *(in complete agreement)* We have.

KEENE. In some ways, I've been living in dread—from the very moment we were married—thinking that sooner or later I'd hear the words, "I'm leaving you. I've found someone else … richer, sexier, more adept at household repairs." Or something. *(Pause)* I've been afraid of saying or doing anything—afraid it might tip the delicate balance. I haven't been brave enough to tell you … to just say out loud … how much I love you. *(Pause)* Why didn't you say something to me?

KIT. There just never seemed to be the right moment—that's all. And then something happened tonight.

KEENE. Two lunatics happened tonight.

KIT. And I had to say what was in my heart or die.

KEENE. Then me, too: Kit, I love you—but we've got an issue.

KIT. I know. And I'm going to show you what a mess I am inside from now on.

KEENE. Not that.

KIT. And we'll work on the competition thing, too.

KEENE. Not that.

KIT. *(with dread after all the surprises of the evening)* Oh, God—what is it?

KEENE. *(with import)* You've always called me Keene.

KIT. That's your name. Isn't it?

KEENE. And only Keene. You've never called me "honey" or "sweetheart" or "darling one." Or something. Like other guys' wives do. Call me crazy and a half—but I've been waiting to hear that from the day we were married. I've been listening so hard to hear that.

KIT. *(sincerely)* If only you'd told me. It may take a little practice, but, honestly, I know I can do it.

KEENE. Let's get married again, Kit.

KIT. Of course. But why?

KEENE. To change our vows and add back in "till death do us part." I've decided that if love is a plane ride, I want a nonstop flight.

(KEENE and KIT look at each other across the space between them—and they realize that the space has grown less lonely. Something catches KIT's eye.)

KIT. Keene, look at the moon! It's growing brighter and brighter. Just for us.

KEENE. That light's not from the moon, Kit. That's … I don't know what that is.

KIT. Well, whatever it is, it's moving toward us …

KEENE: At a very high velocity.

KIT. *(staring straight up)* And it's huge. It's gargantuan. It's … unearthly …

KEENE. *(staring straight up)* And it's hovering over us right now…

(Startling beams of intense white light shoot straight down out of the sky, capturing KIT and KEENE in an illuminated circle. Husband and wife shield their eyes, trying to look up into the source of the light—but the light is too blinding. They look at each other and shrug their shoulders as if to say, "Well, what can we do?" They embrace each other warmly.)

KIT. *(sweetly)* We were thinking about moving anyway.

KEENE. *(joking weakly)* I just hope real estate values outside the Milky Way aren't sky high.

(A strangely beautiful but unearthly music vaguely reminiscent of Mozart fills the air.)

KIT. Maybe there'll be a book in it … honey.

KEENE. *(smiling with satisfaction at her)* Maybe there will be, sweetheart. Maybe there will.

(KIT and KEENE cling tenderly to each other as THE CURTAIN FALLS.)

END OF PLAY

Property Plot (1)

"I'll Take Manhattan"

2 [illegible]iefcases
[illegible]opy of *Time* magazine
a copy of *Highlights for Children* magazine
2 cell phones
2 notebooks
2 pens
2 business cards
coin

Property Plot (2)

"Yes, Sir, That's My Baby"

man's wallet, containing a fold-out string of photographs
dog treats (several for each performance)
2 oversized foam rubber mallets or foam rubber baseball bats

Property Plot (3)

"In Other Words"

telephone
file folder with pages of notes
pen
woman's purse
small handgun
airline airsickness bag
business card
woman's make-up compact
bullet

Property Plot (4)

"Everywhere"

small pocket notebook
pencil
Styrofoam cup
coffee maker

Property Plot (5)

"You Oughta Be in Pictures"

helium-filled balloons
a notebook
a pen
175 pieces of paper that look like one-dollar bills
a piece of Bazooka bubble gum (one for each performance)
a videotape
2 "scripts"—each with six pages stapled together
several hair pins

Property Plot (6)

"They Can't Take That Away From Me"

bottle of champagne
silver wine cooler with ice
4 champagne glasses
bank check
4 straws
drum
sand blocks
musical triangle with accompanying small metal rod
kazoo
remote control (used to adjust outdoor lights)
party whistle that unfurls when blown

COSTUME PLOT (1)

"I'll Take Manhattan"

KIT MARCH
expensive business suit
silk blouse
high heels
conservative earrings
watch
KEENE WINFIELD
expensive business suit
white shirt
conservative tie
dress shoes
watch

COSTUME PLOT (2)

"Yes, Sir, That's My Baby"

DR. DELIA CANTOR
colorful, free-flowing professional skirt and blouse
low-heeled shoes
delicate, nontraditional earrings, necklace, and bracelets
IRA POPOFSKY
wrinkled long-sleeve shirt
wrinkled corduroy pants
wrinkled sports jacket
argyle socks
scuffed loafers

COSTUME PLOT (3)

"In Other Words"

DR. PETER LITTLE
beige shirt
brown, tweed jacket
brown tie
beige slacks
brown belt
beige socks
brown shoes
CARLA PICCOLINO
gray outer coat
gray-blue conservative designer dress
blue-gray shoes with low heels
blue-gray purse

COSTUME PLOT (4)

"Everywhere"

DR. ROBERT KITTLESON
khaki pants
short-sleeve white shirt
black tie
black belt
black shoes
wire-rim glasses
DES RAGE
upscale Hollywood grunge
cowboy boots

COSTUME PLOT (5)

"You Oughta Be in Pictures"

DR. JANE GOLDIN
conservative, dark business suit
pale peach blouse
dark, conservative, low-heeled shoes
dark-rimmed bifocals
CANDY KANE
a pink full-body bunny costume
a matching pink shoulder bag

COSTUME PLOT (6)

"They Can't Take That Away From Me"

DR. KEENE WINFIELD
designer-label summer wear
DR. KIT MARCH
designer-label summer wear
TEDDY MOORE
inexpensive summer wear
bikini bathing suit
DINAH MOORE
inexpensive summer wear
bikini bathing suit

SCENIC DESIGN

"I'LL TAKE MANHATTAN"

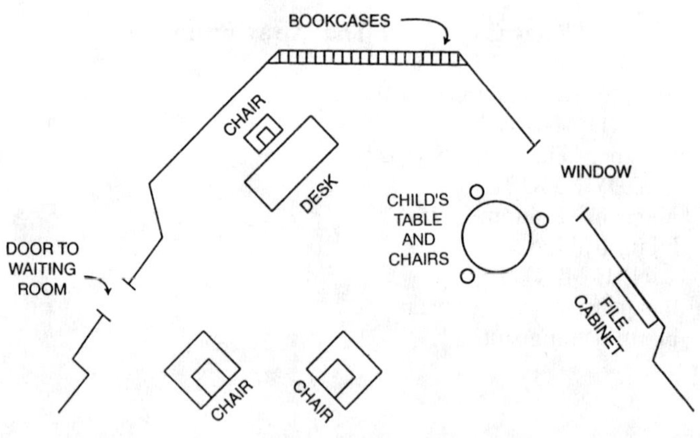

SCENIC DESIGN

"YES, SIR, THAT'S MY BABY"

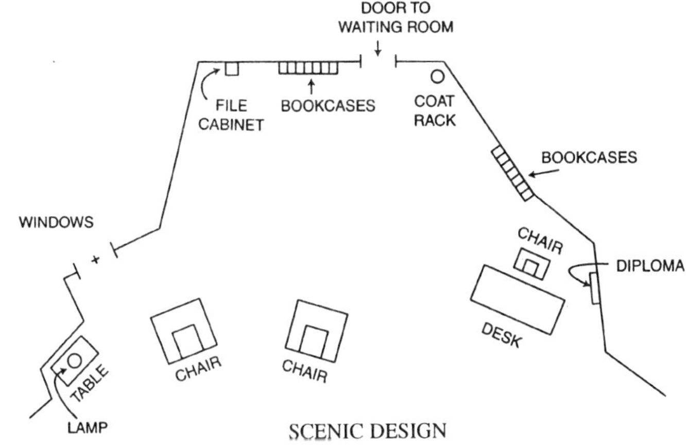

SCENIC DESIGN

"IN OTHER WORDS"

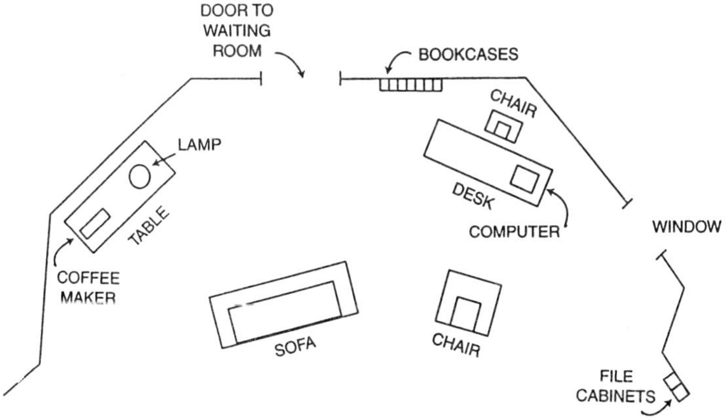

SCENIC DESIGN

"EVERYWHERE"

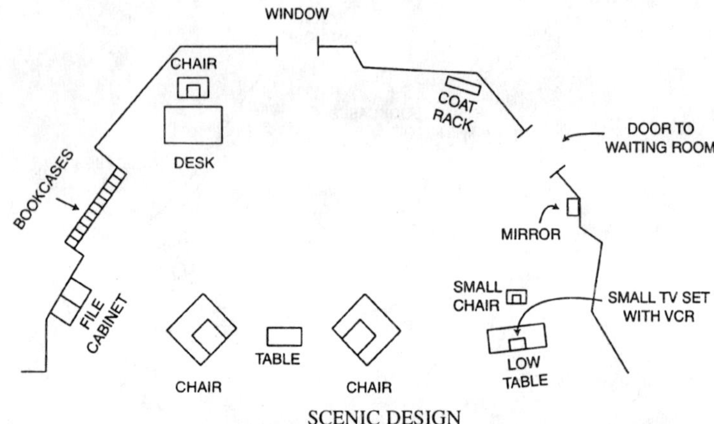

SCENIC DESIGN

"YOU OUGHTA BE IN PICTURES"

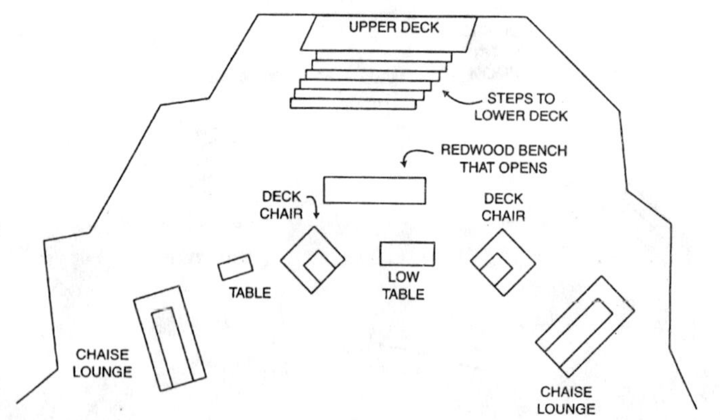

SCENIC DESIGN

"THEY CAN'T TAKE THAT AWAY FROM ME"